BRIDGING THE
G A P

BRIDGING THE
GAP

A Spiritual Journey to Heaven and Back

CALVIN CASSADY

Copyright © 2023 Calvin Cassady.

All rights reserved. No part of this book may be reproduced in any form or by any electronic or mechanical means, including information storage and retrieval systems, without permission in writing from the publisher, except by reviewers, who may quote brief passages in a review.

Library of Congress Control Number: 2023904289

ISBN: 978-1-960093-24-0   (Paperback Edition)
ISBN: 978-1-960093-25-7   (Hardcover Edition)
ISBN: 978-1-960093-26-4   (E-book Edition)

Printed in the United States of America

In Memory

My Mother
Betty Zane Cassady

TABLE OF CONTENTS

Dedication ix
Prologue xi
Introduction xiii

Chapter 1: The Journey Begins 1
Chapter 2: Guardian Angels 10
Chapter 3: To Eternity and Back 12
Chapter 4: Sanctuary 16
Chapter 5: What Are My Options? 26
Chapter 6: Surgery Day 31
Chapter 7: Preparing for the Future 36
Chapter 8: Leaving Sanctuary Behind 42
Chapter 9: From Darkness to Light 44
Chapter 10: Damage Control 49
Chapter 11: College to the Classroom 56
Chapter 12: Leaning on Faith 62
Chapter 13: Fragile! Handle With Care! 67
Chapter 14: Stories from the Classroom 76
Chapter 15: Breaking Point 100
Chapter 16: Down but Not Out 106
Chapter 17: Winds of Change 110
Chapter 18: The Day After 115
Chapter 19: Countdown to Tomorrow 119
Chapter 20: Leap of Faith 122

Chapter 21: One More Trip 127
Chapter 22: Changing Direction 131
Chapter 23: Losing Sight 134
Chapter 24: Turn Around Ranch.. 140
Chapter 25: On the Road Again.. 143
Chapter 26: Broken Hearts 150
Chapter 27: "My Jesus of Mercy, I Trust in You"...................................156

Afterwards 161
About the Author.. 167

DEDICATION

Vicki, my wife and my daughters Sarah and Rebecca

PROLOGUE

At the Easter Sunday service in 2010 God hinted at a new project for me. At the church service the priest spoke about recognizing our God given talents. He spoke of special moments we experience with God in our lives. This was almost forty years after God scraped my body off the asphalt of a curvy Ozark Mountain roadway and allowed me a brief glimpse of his world. That experience was the beginning of a spiritual journey that scanned years as an educator, a church leader, a tornado survivor, and a missionary.

The priest insisted that it was a Christian duty to share these experiences with others. Until that point shared my special times with only small groups, friends and family. This sermon left me trying to decipher God's message.

The next week, the Catholic Bishop addressed our school group and shared the same message. The message was clear, I was to share. I volunteered to be a speaker at the Spring Senior retreat. At that event, following my testimony, I announced my intent to publish this book.

It was God's intervention that accompanied me on my spiritual journey and He was always there to celebrate the good times and to lend support during the challenging times.

God challenged me to share with the world.

I accepted his challenge.

INTRODUCTION

I was just an ordinary teenager. I was in no way an over achieving Christian, but I did believe. I was in no way associated with preparation for church work. I was just an uptight college kid looking for a new direction. I had no intention of being a messenger of God

Then one spring day in 1971 I was on a day outing to an area amusement park with my two best friends. We were all in college and while we had varied backgrounds and varied interests, we enjoyed each other's company. The events of the next twenty four hours would change and define my life forever.

It was an unexplained automobile accident that occurred on a curvy Ozark mountain highway. The impact caused the car to burst into flames and plunged me into a clouded existence that included a walk through the valley of the shadow of death and I emerged on the threshold of eternal life. While eternity surrounded me and filled me with an absolute certainty of heaven, I walked away. I walked away because I was not satisfied with my earthly service. I was assured that I was accepted unconditionally into the eternal kingdom, but I could see a future with an opportunity to fulfill the service gap.

Following a miraculous recovery, and a lot of guidance from my parents and a loving relationship with my soon to be wife, I completed my college training in three years and continued my journey as an elementary school teacher. It wasn't long until my "gift" could be shared. That was the beginning a thirty year career in education that offered numerous opportunities to use my new God given talents. During my teaching years I was blessed by the marriage to my wife, Vicki and the birth of my two daughters, Rebecca and Sarah.

It was also during these early years that I had a role in my local church. I served in many capacities but was most proud of the 11 years I served as youth minister. During those years I spent a lot of time working and ministering to young people in middle school through high school. Using my position I presented my story in the context of the church. It was well received by the youth. Following a change in church leadership and the calling of a new priest I was asked to resign my position without a reason or cause. This was a very disturbing time, but prayer allowed me to set this aside. I continued my work quietly in the schools.

Other challenges occurred along the way but my first faith shaking experience in my new life occurred when my mother died suddenly in an automobile accident. I had spent the last ten years helping others through this kind of tragedy but now I was to experience the need for that kind of assistance.

The depth of grief was doubled by the fact that my father was driving the car, blamed himself, and was consumed with guilt. In the twinkle of an eye I was losing the foundation of my family. It became clear now that it was part of God's plan that I set aside my church duties. I needed to allow myself time to grieve.

This event strengthened my spiritual foundation. With God's help I survived this bump in the road and continued on my journey with an even greater persistence and conviction. After my mom's passing I knew I was placed here for a special reason.

I completed my career in public education in 2002. This was a difficult year for the nation with the destruction of the World Trade Center and I had weathered some personal difficulties that year. My wife and I both retired from teaching in the public schools. We felt the need for a new direction.

The following years were full of changes. My oldest daughter Rebecca was zeroing in on her teaching degree, engaged and married. My youngest, Sarah was taking her first teaching position and it wasn't long until my first grandson Calvin arrived. A short time later God blessed us with the birth of my second grandson Wilson. There is nothing more spiritual then grandchildren.

For me the next year was a struggle to find an existence. I enjoyed the role of "pappy", the name the grand-boys selected for me, but I missed the fulfillment of a ministry. I did some work substituting but that was different. I was working with different kids each day. Not enough time to "make a difference.

The Sunday after Easter in April of 2003 I sat in a church pew listening to the priest talk about changes in our lives, and finding God's purpose for our lives. This was troubling because I thought I knew what I was to do for God. That day I knelt and prayed that God would change my life and help me define his goals for me.

Later that evening, after attending a Mexico mission trip meeting I returned home to find most of my house destroyed by a killer tornado that struck our community. A new chapter in my spiritual journey of growth and service was opening.

Since that day in May 2003, my Christian journey has taken me to Mexico on two mission trips. I have weathered potential high anxiety health events involving my brain, my heart, and my vision. After each scare I thanked the Lord and I knew that there was more of my journey.

I was employed as a teacher in a Regional Catholic High School for five years. I rejoiced the opportunity to again serve young people. I also ventured into the realm of adult ministry. I have launched a blog that chronicles the presence of God in my daily life.

I have also recently been blessed with the opportunity to have knee replacement surgery and cataract surgery on both eyes. Ironically these are the areas that were most damaged in the 1971 automobile accident.

There it is. That's how it happened. The story that follows connects the dots. It "Bridges the Gaps" of my life and more importantly "Bridges the Gap" between our earthly existence and our spiritual destination.

CHAPTER 1

THE JOURNEY BEGINS

It was a crisp clear spring morning. It was the 28th day of May in 1971. Mom and dad left for work as usual, my mom was an elementary school teacher and my dad was a junior high guidance counselor in Joplin, Missouri.

I was having some reservations about the day's activities. I was not totally honest with my parents as I had reported a day trip to the lake. That is all I said. There was an assumption that we would be fishing on Grand Lake in Northeast Oklahoma about forty-five minutes from my house in Joplin. In truth, we were planning to visit a Midwest amusement park west of Branson, Missouri.

While I was dealing with my anxiety, a brand-new Ford Mustang rolled up in front of my house. I dismissed my uneasiness for the moment and welcomed my friends. After a walk around and some comments of admiration for Stan's "new wheels," I climbed into the back seat and settled in for the first leg of our trip. I was picked up last and just took the back seat as a convenience. Don was the front seat passenger. We made our way through town feeling for a "day of freedom."

As we pulled onto I-44, I countered my feelings of guilt with the knowledge that we were not skipping school today, there were no classes. Ironically, it was "dead day" a day when there were no classes or activities scheduled. It was to be a day to spend in the library or at home studying for finals that would begin on Tuesday. Monday we would celebrate Memorial Day.

For me this activity was the finale of a school year that left me feeling like giving up. I had been pressured by my family to take overloaded schedules and summer school classes, allowing me to graduate from college a year early. That sounded good in the beginning, but at this stage I hated going to school. I did turn in my projects, but I was counting on my finals to pull me though. I was a good test taker. All may have been saved, but the finals weren't going to happen.

Stan, the driver, and Don were two of my best friends. We had gone to high school together for two years. During our senior year we were separated when the city opened a new high school. Don went to Memorial and Stan and I continued at Joplin High School, now named Parkwood High School.

After graduation we were reunited at Missouri Southern College, a new four-year institution in Joplin. None of us were overjoyed with the idea of staying home for college and truthfully Don and Stan weren't really overjoyed with the whole idea of college. It was clubs and activities that made college life acceptable. Don and I had an interest in music and enjoyed being in the college band. It was on the marching field that I met my wife, Vicki. I was involved in student government and was president of the junior class. All three of us were committee-member of the college union board with Vicki. We were also all involved in college political clubs.

The road sign showed the next exit was Sarcoxie. We still had 53 miles to Springfield, our first stop. It was a beautiful spring day and it was already warming up. We were moving on down the highway, road testing that new white pony. Our comments were random as we jumped from one subject to another. The mood was light as we moved on with our adventure.

Don, the front seat passenger, and I met during my sophomore year at what was then Joplin High School. That was my first year in Joplin as our family had relocated so my father could take a job as a guidance counselor. Don's parents and mine were friends on a professional level as they were also members of the teaching profession. Don's dad was an elementary school principal and his mom Dora was an elementary school teacher.

His parents were those people in my life that would fill in when things in my own home world were cloudy. I spent many afternoons with Don at his house, one of the diversions from my classes. We did a lot a running together. Don had a younger sister and with him in college, the sister's life was in the spotlight. That didn't seem to bother Don much. He and his dad were two of the most laid back individuals that I have ever met.

I don't think he was anxious about the day's activities like I was because he had a more open relationship with his parents than I did. He was allowed to make choices for himself. I can't say they were always the best choices but making decisions is a life skill. When one makes the choices one also, must understand that there are consequence and responsibilities that go with the decisions. As a career goal Don was pretty much uncommitted, but leaned toward an education major.

I don't know what he told his parents about the day's activities but I knew we all were to be home by 5:30.

We were reaching our exit and the Shoney's sign was in sight. We were all hungry as we had not eaten breakfast. We all liked to eat. Eating lunch out was a trademark for this threesome. We had eaten at every restaurant in the four states and what if it did run over into my afternoon class schedule. That was another one of my sinful diversions that kept me from reaching my pre-established goals.

The only goal that mattered now was the buffet line. Pancakes and eggs and don't forget the sausage and bacon. I believe they even had ham. My favorite was the biscuits and gravy. We enjoyed a little strawberry shortcake to finish up.

We talked as we ate about the next part of the adventure. Truthfully we would not have much time to spend at the amusement park as we had to be home by 5:30. We had all been to this amusement park on a high school outing when we were juniors. At that time the park was in its infant stage. Since then, it had undergone its first real expansion with new rides.

Calvin Cassady

It was just opening for the season and we planned to experience as much as possible.

With full stomachs we were ready for the hour plus ride through Branson to our destination. We all climbed into the car and the front seat passengers snapped their seat belts. This was the beginning of an era when all car came with factory equipped seatbelts. The car also was equipped with high back seats with head rests. This was supposed to be a safety item as well as adding to the comfort of the front seat passengers.

The new seat design probably did add an element of safety if the back seat passengers were belted in behind the high back front seats, but what kind of social exchange could occur if you were in the back. I opted to ride in the middle of the back seat free from the seat belt. This enabled me to see what was going on and participate in the dialogue.

The next part of the trip was a bit more of a challenge as the highway between Springfield and Branson was only two lanes. There were steep grades and curvy cut backs as we went up and down the Ozark hills.

We fashioned ourselves as masters of the road and one of our dream projects was to organize a road race. We spent afternoons driving the country side looking for an acceptable road racing course. That was another of the diversions that haunted me.

With the roads as they were it would take a full hour to reach the city of Branson.

As the rubber of the tires met the challenges of the road ahead, my mind returned to thoughts of dishonesty and while I had not told a lie, I knew that what I was doing was wrong. But what could I do? I couldn't back out now. We were almost to our destination. We just had to be home by 5:30. If we made it back I could avoid talk of the day and still not have to lie. If we could just get home on time everything would be OK.

Stan, the driver, lived at home with his mother Mary and his brother Charley. Mary was a registered nurse. Stan's dad was in the military and had died. I never knew the story, but a picture of his father was proudly displayed at his house. One of his main interests in high school was ROTC. He was very dedicated to that activity. This activity instilled responsibility and leadership. That's why Ma Mary could depend on Stan and his brother to help maintain their household. That is why he probably had less anxiety over today because he seemed to make many of his own decisions.

We became friend in high school and when we hooked up in college we just continued where we left off. We played intramural sports together. Stan was the one with the athletic build. I was on the varsity tennis team and in season I was in good shape, but Stan worked out year round and maintained his broad shouldered muscular build. Don was not real athletic and he really didn't care. His blonde hair would flash in the sunlight and his sparkling disposition allowed him to enjoy life one minute at a time. With his attitude about life I doubt if he had any reservations about the day.

As we exited off Highway 65 and onto Highway 76 we pulled onto a narrow two lane roadway. We started to think about our time restraints. We were only a few miles from our destination but to accomplish it we would have to navigate some of the most dangerous miles of public road in the state of Missouri. When you factor in thirty to forty minutes to reach our destination our time at the amusement park was limited to just over two hours. What a depressing thought considering all the miles behind us and those still ahead.

We crept through the narrow streets on the west side of that sleepy Ozark mountain community and we began to see signs telling us our journey's end was near. It could have been my imagination but our pace seemed to have picked up a little as we charged up and down hills and careened around curves taking up more than our share of the lonely mountain road. Stan was an aggressive driver who liked to attack the road, but he did nothing that day that would cause alarm.

I can't complain about his driving as he taught me most of my behind the wheel maneuvers and I was looking forward to taking my driving test in his car in the next few weeks. Yes, I was one of those poor sheltered youngsters whose father refused to allow him to get a driver's license. It would just be another diversion that would distract me from reaching my goals.

The road stretched out in front of us as we sped past Shepherd of the Hills, a tourist attraction and outdoor theater showcasing the book by the same name. Signs for Silver Dollar City were more frequent and beckoning us on. As we passed Old Matt's Cabin, a part of Shepherd of the Hills, we slammed on our brake and our car horn shattered the silence of the spring midday quiet. A dog had crossed our path, or rather we crossed his path and we slowed allowing him to continue on his reckless way.

That's the last thing I remember prior to the accident. The doctors say the trauma of the event erased from my mind the last minutes before the impact. The following explanation of the accident was derived from accounts offered by Stan and Don and from the accident report filed by the Missouri Highway Patrol.

The accident occurred eight miles west of Branson in Stone County just inside the county line. The highway patrol reported that the accident happened around 11:30 a.m. It occurred when the car I was a passenger in crossed the center line and left the roadway. The car then hit a concrete culvert, bounced and slammed head-on into a tree. The tree kept the car from plummeting over an embankment and spiraling to the bottom of a deep roadside ravine. The bounce caused a gas leak that resulted in an explosion and fire. The car burned in a matter of minutes.

Stan and Don managed to get out of the car with the assistance of two men who were following us in a truck and witnessed the accident. They also assisted in removing me from the wreckage. They were able to pull us all out of harm's way just seconds before the explosion. In a short time that brand new automobile was nothing more than a pile of charred metal.

Why did the accident occur? Were we just a bunch of stoned teenagers out for a joy ride? Let's set the record straight. There was no evidence of substance abuse, neither alcohol nor drugs. The accident could have occurred when the midday sun reflecting off the hood blinded the driver. It could have occurred because of a mechanical defect in car. There were some factory defects discovered in some cars of that model. There was not enough of the car left to tell if it was caused by a factory defect. The recklessness of our ages could have been a contributing factor, but the lack of evidence could not support a degree of cause. We know that the speed of car was slowed to avoid hitting the dog. So what are we left with? There was no conclusive cause. It was just an accident.

* * * * *

A quick accident scene assessment of personal injury suggested that Stan, the driver, had suffered a severe arm injury. Don's injury seemed to be in his back but the severity was not detected at the scene. There was little talk about my condition.

I remember lying near the roadway. My head was wrapped with something. Later I found it was a T-shirt from one of the rescuers. I remember the heat and the crackling from car fire and I remember being confused. I remember a dark, shirt was covering my eyes. I remember the shirt was heavy and wet, from gushing blood.

Something that I have never really understood was the fact that in my memory this whole event took place in darkness, if I didn't know better I would have reported it at night and maybe in the late fall as it seemed cool. In truth it was midday, sunny and warm in late May. In reality I was in and out of consciousness after I was removed from the wreckage.

I remember being rolled to the ambulance. I can vaguely remember the ride. The gurney was moving back and forth as the vehicle shifted gear and seemed to be clinging to the hilly, curvy terrain in route to Skaggs Hospital in Branson. I remember being rushed into the hospital only to return to the ambulance for another trip.

Later I understand that the emergency room doctor at Branson sent me on with the ambulance driver because he felt there was little they could do for me there and the assumption was that I would die.

Stan the driver was taken by ambulance to St. John's Hospital in Springfield, Missouri. He had a badly broken arm, but was in a room by the time his mother arrived at the hospital. He heard early reports of my grave condition and he said that he cried uncontrollably.

Don was admitted to the hospital in Branson with non-life-threatening injuries. He also understood that I had died in the ambulance on the way to St. Johns Hospital in Springfield. Later he was in for a big surprise as was the attending physician from the Branson hospital.

* * * * *

Truthfully, I did die in the ambulance in route to the hospital in Springfield. What my traveling friends didn't know was that I returned to life. The ambulance attendants knew that I was clinically dead and that I was revived. I don't know to this day if the resuscitation was shock related or chemically induced. The story of that time overlaps into the spiritual/emotional realm and will be addressed in a later chapter.

* * * * *

When I arrived at St. Johns hospital in Springfield it was early afternoon. I had suffered a severe head laceration in which 75% of the scalp was detached from the skull. This left the skull and all the nerve endings and capillaries exposed and a target for infection. The cut interrupted blood flow to and from the brain. The skull remained unbroken. It did its job and protected the brain. There was no concussion.

After some tense moments in the emergency room, the huge scalp laceration was closed and a neurologist and the ER team were able to address the extent of damage. The main problem and concern of the ER doctors was that on the way to the hospital, my blood level plunged below a lethal level resulting in the stoppage of the heart. The combination of events resulted in a clinical death. There was a probability of brain damage due to a deprivation of oxygen from the lack of blood. An accurate account of the time the brain suffered oxygen deprivation was unavailable.

Once in the ER, doctors were able to do extensive testing and determined that all the brain functions were normal. The team of doctors confirmed the brain was not damaged. The young Asian neurologist told my parents and later told me that I was "no worse" than before the accident.

With the head injury stabilized the ER staff next examined the leg injury. There was extreme damage to the left femur. The limb was fractured and six inches of the bone was crushed when the inertia of the car caused the leg to become trapped behind the high back seat and then slammed forward when the car hit the tree. The crash left a six inches gap in the bone above my knee and below the joint at the hip. Because of the missing bone and the trauma involved with the accident as a whole there was a real possibility that I might lose my leg.

My total body was damaged. Would it become stronger? Was my traumatized immune system strong enough to fight off all of the possibilities of infection? The next 24-36 hours were critical. Those crucial hours were spent in the intensive care unit.

I remember a brief visit with my parent on that Friday evening. I remember that I was not conscious enough to know that the major damage was to my leg and my head. I remember the bright lights of the intensive care unit and the repetitive noises from all of the monitors. I had feelings that there had been an accident. My whole experience in ICU remains foggy.

Needless to say, I didn't get home on that Friday evening by 5:30 p.m.

CHAPTER 2

GUARDIAN ANGELS

Guardian Angels are thought to be spiritual beings that are "assigned" to assist people here on earth in various ways. Whether there is one angel per person, one angel for several persons or several angels for one person is open to question. What is their assignment?

It is believed that they intercept at many junctures in our lives and help, whenever they can make our lives run more smoothly. Sometimes this is by inspiring a thought to spur us to action, or at another it is to lend us super human strength, or a third to remove us from harm's way. There are many instances in our lives which are put down to luck, coincidence or even miracles, but which have the touch of a hand behind it.

What does this talk of "guardian angels" have to do with my story? Remember the crash occurred and the car burned and three injured young men had to escape. Remember, I was in the back seat of a two door vehicle. Remember I mentioned the passerby's or the rescuers. This is their story.

There were two men who immediately happened on the accident scene. They said they were right behind us and witnessed the wreck. Stan did not recall seeing the truck in his rear-view mirror. They must have been close behind though because the car exploded almost immediately after impact.

The men had no names. They were driving an unidentified utility truck. The truck driver was trained in CPR and first aid. His passenger was a hitch-hiker. He was member of the clergy who was being delivered to an undisclosed location.

The strangers worked quickly and together to remove us from the car that was a "dripping time bomb". They moved us to a secure location just off the roadway. As the truck driver worked diligently to stabilize our injuries and stop the bleeding from my gaping head laceration, the passenger offered prayer on our behalf. Feeling satisfied that they had done all that was necessary; these mystery men disappeared as quickly as they had appeared.

A message was received by both the highway patrol and the ambulance personnel but both arrived at an accident scene with a smoldering automobile shell and three lonely accident victims suffering besides the roadways. By this time, the rescuers were gone.

There was little official evidence as to the cause of the accident. It has been impossible to verify the presence of our mystery rescuers on that day.

I have since tried. There was a record of the accident being radioed in from the accident scene. This message summoning help was received by both the highway patrol and the ambulance crew but in both cases the name of the caller was not available.

The only evidence of their existence was from Stan and Don and Me. The highway patrol did not pursue their presence and recorded in their accident report that the passengers apparently were able to free themselves from the vehicle before it burned. If we had not received assistance we would have been burned inside the car.

I think you can see that these circumstances are nothing short of a miracle and you can understand why I refer to the two strangers as "Our Guardian Angels."

CHAPTER 3

TO ETERNITY AND BACK

What happens when you die? How does one transcend from mankind to heavenly being, from the known to the eternal mysteries. The following is an account of the emotional and spiritual happenings just prior to and during my trip to heaven.

My personal feelings associated with the early part of this day were guilt and fear.

While I did not lie about my activities, I was not completely truthful. There was always the possibility that I could be caught. This activity was the culmination of a semester of bitter attitudes. It was designed as an escape or release from my frustrations. This trip was the source of increasing anxiety. From the moment of the accident my emotional state plunged to feelings of shame, of helplessness and of despair. Time and space disappeared and a growing sense of anticipation followed the roadside scene and accompanied me in the ambulance. This feeling of anticipation grew until my heart stops beating.

My transition started with a sharp decrease in energy. The fear and guilt remained. Initially this event was submerged in a creepy dark, cold environment. As I breathed my last breath, of human consciousness it was immediately replaced with a spiritual consciousness.

I was aware of a closure and a transition. My spirit spiraled through the dark cold emptiness. My life unfolded before me in small bright episodes. I was aware of a presence, a judgment, THE JUDGEMENT. Anxiety continued to rise. I awaited the revelations of my sinful acts and of the flaws of my inner character. My fear and my guilt peaked. My spirit tumbled through space at a rapid speed. While movement was apparent, direction and distance were unknown and time as a sense of measure disappeared.

Suddenly, the cold, dark confusion was replaced with a settling of increasing light. While each episode of my life was revealed, the light and warmth increased until I emerged in an atmosphere of radiant beams and a bright, welcoming coziness. The feelings of guilt, of fear and of anxiousness were replaced with feelings of peace, of tranquility and of hope.

Where were my sinful acts of the past? What about my less than perfect inner character? I didn't argue about it. I was just relieved. At this point I was more concerned with my lack of accomplishment. Where was the good? Was that my life? Was that all?

I was well aware of two distinct places. One was familiar, one was unfamiliar. As I stood on the threshold of this new dimension, a gentle breeze filled my being with knowledge of forgiveness, of grace, of acceptance, and of unconditional love. I tried to sort it all out.

Where was I? Was what I thought was happening to me actually happening to me? What about sin? What about life? What about death?

Then in cadence with the proceeding an invitation was received. Not written. Not spoken. It was dictated through the heart.

"You may enter the kingdom of heaven, for he who believeth in me shall not parish but shall have everlasting life?"

Just like that. Unconditionally! No sin! Built on belief! Just as I am! I was young, my opportunity for service was limited, but my faith was strong.

Before I could make a commitment, it was as if a huge curtain rose and in this radiant light I stood on the threshold of eternity.

Heaven spread before me. At first it was very quiet. My brief heavenly encounter didn't include human contact. There was no evidence of a spoken language. All of the messaging on this occasion was a non-verbal form and dictated through my heart.

My eyes were filled with the imagery of spring. It was early morning, the dawn of a new time. The natural heavenly light revealed mountain woodlands. A meadow of various grasses, dotted with wildflowers, stretched to the edge of the woods. A sparkling stream of cool, clear water meandered through the landscape. A variety of trees, of different sizes and species, are intermixed with other woodland foliage. The scene was vivid; the colors were vibrant and pure. In the distance mountain ranges rose to the sky and reached through the clouds.

My ears were treated to enhanced sounds of nature. There was the sound of running water moving naturally. Ripples broke the surface with a splash. Grasses and trees rustled in the breezes. Birds and other sounds of the natural world were filtered for purist reception.

I was not an observer I was a part of this wholeness.

There was that perfect freshness of the air. It was warmed by the natural light yet cooled by the breezes. That air carried mixed aromas blending the fragrances of pine, spruce, and cedar with the sweet smells of the blooming wildflowers.

It was a scene of total tranquility. Pure and inviting; Irresistible! Then again the invitation and the assurance of it genuineness was offered.

I had arrived!

Yet as I stood before the master and all his creation, I remained troubled with my vision and the life that I brought with me. I began to feel a source of emptiness and a need for fulfillment. I understood that I was young and my opportunity for service was limited. I felt this strong desire to serve.

While the love for those I left behind was painful, that was not primary in my request to remain on earth; my request to serve was stronger. The bonus of newly acquired knowledge made service possibilities even greater. While Heaven surrounded me and filled my being with an absolute certainty of eternal life, I walked away.

As I began to return I immediately felt the purity of the moment fade as perfection slipped back to a flawed and sin filled world. As quickly as I had arrived, I was returned.

My life on earth would never be the same.

So now what?

It's all good?

Not so fast. An absolute knowledge, not just faith, doesn't assure anything. The reason is choice. I can't complain and I can only speak for my own experience but it was choice that brought me back. Judgment is not only about sin, but it is also about the total package. People have a choice right up to the very end.

I've always wondered why some people on death's bed rally and return and others pass without incident. I also wondered why the moment of death always seems to be relaxed and accepting. Now I know. Now I can better understand. A lot has to do with how you view your judgment and the life you live. You have that free choice right up to the end.

CHAPTER 4

SANCTUARY

I stared into a bright light. My head was locked in place. All I could see was the light. In the background I could hear a tone, a beeping, continuing tone, over and over again.

I felt like a large boulder had smashed my chest. No pain, just a heavy feeling.

Out of the light I felt a touch, a warm, gentle touch.

I heard a soft comforting voice, "Get closer, He can't move. He can't turn to see you. Remember, he is very medicated. He should be able to see you. Don't expect too much."

Into the light came a comforting view of mom. I slowly connected the touch with the face.

I heard this far away but familiar voice, "Buster, can you hear me?"

While I tried to respond, I was too far from conscious to make sense. Maybe it was an eye blink or an arm jerk. It was something; something that caused mom's face to lose some of its fear and anxiousness. Her expression radiated hope but concern and confusion remained. I felt the touch become a tight grip on my right hand. My mom was a strong woman even in the face of adversity.

She spoke again, "Don't worry honey, it's going to be all right."

As she released my hand my mind started to slide back towards sleep. Just before my consciousness faded I saw my dad. He bent over and looked down. He was speechless. Dads aren't as good at covering up as moms. His face was ash gray and stained with tears. It mirrored feelings of hurt and fear.

That was all.

The hospital reported my condition as serious. Everything appeared to be stable. They would re-evaluate my condition in forty-eight hours. The hospital staff cautioned my parents that the next twenty-four hours would determine if I was to live or die, and would provide clues to what my recovery would look like and the quality of life that I could expect.

* * * * *

For the next thirty-six hours. I remained in a semi-conscious state in the Intensive Care Unit at St. John's Hospital in Springfield, Missouri. This restful time allowed the antibiotics to try and counter all of the possibilities of infection. Another concern was the condition of the heart. The accident had caused it great trauma and my survival depended on its ability to rebound. The body needed several blood transfusions during that quiet healing period.

The orthopedic team headed by a doctor who was willing to be creative and take a chance, placed the left leg in traction to try and stabilize the fractured area of the left femur. A look at the x-rays revealed six inches of missing bone, ground to dust in the accident. The bone couldn't be set. There was too much missing. The best they could was to keep it stable.

The neurologists continued to monitor the huge head laceration for any signs of infection. The stitches that held the cut together were large, random and sporadic indicating the need for speed to close the wound. The doctor joked saying he had to hand stitch it, the Singer was Out of Order. The head wound was dressed and wrapped with white gauze in a mummy fashion.

While the doctors were working, and I was resting, my parents were praying, really praying. I'm not sure how they got the news of the accident.

They were still in school. Arrangements had to be made so they could relocate to Springfield. Driving back and fourth was too much, especially when every second counted.

There were questions that no one had answers for. The Highway Patrol report was vague and while it could not offer a cause for the accident, it silently assessed blame to the driver.

Fortunately, for now, love trumped blame and no energy was wasted on deciding who was at fault. Stan's insurance company agreed up front to pay for the medical bills, yet no fault was admitted or assessed.

* * * * *

The accident happened on a Friday about noon. It is now Sunday evening. I was moved to a four bed orthopedic ward just before noon on Sunday morning. I rested peacefully and awoke on my own when mom spoke.

She again drew near the bed and whispered, "Wake Up, Sleepy Head!"

I knew that voice. It was strong and close. I was still confused. Where am I? My thoughts quickly drifted back to the words. I knew they were spoken by my mother. I had heard them before. I'd heard them often. They usually meant I was late. I opened my eyes and they met mom's bright cheerful smile.

True the smile was masking looks of concern, but relief seemed to be the general mood. I tried to lift my head. It was not restrained but I simply didn't have the energy. I looked past my mom and standing behind her was my father. He looked considerably better than the last time I saw him.

"He-l-l-o," He murmured.

That's his standard greeting. This time it was his grip that latched onto my arm. He was holding tight as if he might not let go.

"You made it." You made it," he continued.

I was still very unsure as to what was happening. I did notice that the bright lighting was gone and I actually saw some natural light coming from a window across the room. The room was quiet.

Mom bent over and kissed my cheek.

"Don't worry; you're going to be all right. You just rest. Daddy and I will be right here." Mom's comments trailed off.

That was it for Sunday. It was a short episode, but in a small way things were starting to become familiar. I drifted back to sleep.

* * * * *

My parents had remained at the hospital until I was out of the woods. My condition improved rapidly during the night on Friday and my vital signs returned to normal by midday on Saturday. The scary part was over. The doctors indicated to them that I was out of immediate danger. The hospital staff insisted that they get some rest and take care of any immediate business.

My parents reluctantly returned to Joplin sometime on Saturday. The first order of business was to explain the situation to my brother. Tom was four years younger than I and a sophomore in high school. He had spoken to my parents on the phone but was in need of some reassurance.

Plans were made for him to stay with my grandparents in Sallisaw, Oklahoma during my hospital stay. I regret that Tom did not get to see me until many days later and I know he was frightened and felt left out. My grandparents shared his unhappiness. Tom knew that with the situation as it was, my father's decisions had to be respected, so he obeyed without question.

Mom and dad returned to the hospital Sunday morning prepared to stay in Springfield as long as needed. While they were waiting for me to wake up, one of the nurses asked them if they had a place to stay.

She recommended a lady who had a house not far from the hospital who rented rooms to family members of recovering patients. This was like a private sector Ronald McDonald House. This arrangement was very affordable and very convenient and I thank God for her generosity.

Sunday evening I was introduced to a routine that would continue for the next 10 days.

Methods for delivery of meds was much less advanced then than today and most narcotic painkiller had to be administered by injection. The doctors' orders also included additional antibiotics. The time schedule for injections was every four hours, 24-7. That a lot of shots, two at a time, six times a day. The nurse would hit me with an antibiotic injection. Then, since I was awake; I received a pain shot to put me back to sleep. That routine began on Sunday evening. I received those injections three times during the night.

The nurses told me that beginning with the first injections I slept with one eye opened. That is probably true because I was nineteen years old and had never been hospitalized before. I had never had any medical procedures more invasive than a shot. I was trying to keep track of what was happening to me. By Monday night I was used to the routine.

My parents seemed to be in those same seats next to the bed every time I awoke during the day. Truthfully, I was probably only awake during those early days for just a few minutes. At night I would return to sleep immediately following the pain shot. I was unaware of most activities in those early days of my recovery. My parents were there every day. There may have been other visitors, but I only remember small talk. That was all I had to offer. I felt the need to be polite.

* * * * *

Tuesday morning brought a revised routine. I could tell things were changing following my 4:00 a.m. meds. My plan was to return to sleep so I would be ready to greet my parents at 8:00 a.m.; but the activity level around me would not allow restful sleep.

At 6:30 a.m., still early by my current schedule, I was awakened and introduced to a person from physical therapy. I might mention that hospital protocol seemed to require announcements in regard to my condition be at this hour of the day.

Up to this point I had been laying flat on my back and had been getting all my nourishment from an IV bag. The light came on in my little corner of the room and I was about to become mobile, as mobile as one might become who is in traction.

I really hadn't even explored this whole traction, hospital bed situation. Up to now I didn't have a reason to care. The stuff in my last shot must have been different because I was now alert, a bit anxious, and excited about something new.

Getting on with this mobility exercise, the therapist explained that it was necessary that I exercise what I could of my body to keep my muscles from losing all of their tone. He pointed to a bar on chains hanging above and in front of me. It looked like a trapeze in the circus. Next, I was introduced to the button on the bed that would raise and lower my back. In a matter of seconds I was sitting up in bed. I must admit I was a little faint, but after what I had been through it was not even worth mentioning.

The presence of that bar was a source of curiosity. Not for long. The exercise the therapist was proposing required me to lift my arms up and out, grab the bar and lift myself up. We practiced. The instructions were simple as was the task, but in the days since the wreck my muscles had already lost most of their strength. This task was hard, it was a challenge, and it was required several times during the day.

I wasn't too worried, though I was the only one who knew about this exercise and these instructions.

I might be more alert, but I had a lot to learn about hospital life.

That was a huge load to dump on me at that hour of the day. As the therapist retreated I was ready to return to my horizontal position and get on with my recovery. The problem was the button to recline me was not within my reach. It didn't matter anyway because my nurse had returned with a narrow table on wheels that extended over the bed. She raised it to a comfortable height.

Then she asked, "Are You Hungary?"

That's an interesting question and one I hadn't addressed since the Shoney's experience. The food in a bag had satisfied my cravings up to this point, but when she banged a tray with food down in front of me my appetite returned.

Guess what!

What was on the tray was not what my appetite envisioned. That really didn't matter either. The brain functions that control the motor skills necessary for feeding one's self were a little rusty, and oatmeal, jello and juice were more than I was ready for. Just when the excitement of the moment had peaked, the nurse plunked a huge plastic cup filled with ice and water on the table and demanded that I drink it full at least three times daily.

My tiny taste of independence came to a crashing halt when the nurse, after watching me wrestle with the food for what seemed like forever, suggested that she would feed me and she reached for a spoon.

How hungry was I?

I resisted. I wasn't about to let a total stranger feed me like a baby.

I heard approaching voices from, the hall and as the visitors entered the room I heard that familiar voice, my mom,

"You have to eat if you expect to ever get out of here," she preached.

I was so glad mom and dad were here. At that moment I felt so helpless, so guilty. I was so sorry. Emotions came rushing in and I felt like crying. Mom held me and comforted me as I allowed days of uncertainty and frustration to pour out in the form of tears.

My dad looked on helplessly. These last few days had taken a toll on him. After a few minutes I settled. Mom wiped by face carefully. It was still a mass of scabs and bruises and I had no idea what had happened to me. Dad patted me on the back and we even ate some breakfast together. There's a huge difference in being fed by your mother and in being fed by a stranger, even if she was one of the most kind and caring nurses that cared for me.

It was only 7:00 a.m. but from that moment on my hospital experience took on a whole new direction. Things were starting to make sense. There was more awake time than sleep. Activity was slowly replacing rest. Questions, however, still out numbered answers.

This day was young and there was much more to come. By now there was sunshine filtering through the window and the general lights in the room replaced the focused light over my bed. It was time for my 8:00 med. As the nurse approached, I realized for the first time that my clothes were missing, and this stranger was reaching for the blanket.

She raised the sheet and to my relief I was protected by a thin flimsy hospital gown. The nurse rolled me and gently injected meds into my hip which I'm sure now resembled a pin cushion.

Mom noticed a flash of modesty and explained that until after surgery, I would have to make do with the gown. The traction presented a problem when it came to pajamas. The medicine was quickly taking effect and the modesty issues and all the other adjustments of the moment quickly faded into a restful sleep.

* * * * *

Unlike the sleep of the previous hospital days I was somewhat aware of what was going on around me and while I experienced many hours of REM sleep the nurses still teased that I always had one eye open.

About two hours into my morning nap I awoke to voices. As I opened both eyes I saw my parents visiting quietly at the foot of my bed with a man who appeared to be a doctor. Noticing my eyes were open my mom introduced the man as my neurologist. She raised my bed so I could get a better look. The man was short; he was of Asian descent and seemed very sure of himself.

"Let's have a look," he replied. Pointing to my head, he continued, "You see?"

His nurse produced a mirror and for the first time I experienced the effects of the accident I had no recollection of. My mom drew near and held my arm tightly as I grabbed for the mirror to get a look.

My first impression was very graphic. My complexion was pale. My face was marred with scratches and scabs. My eyes were bruised and swollen. As my look continued upward I spied a head wrapped in white gauze with splatters of blood that soaked through. While I was getting a first look, the doctor produced scissors from his coat and began clipping away at the gauze and unwrapping them in dramatic fashion.

My next look was even more ominous. The last wrap of gauze disappeared revealing a huge cut. It was held together by giant black threads applied in a sporadic, jagged fashion. The stitched area started over one ear and crossed down over my forehead and ended over the other ear. Noticing the shocked confusion on my face the doctor offered the following explanation.

"Your head hit hard in the accident." He explained. "It split just like a melon. Singer sewing machine broke down; I had to sew by hand. You like," he continued.

He next spoke to my folks.

"Mr. and Mrs. Cassady, Your son is no worse off than before the accident," he concluded.

He fashioned himself a comedian of sorts. While his nurse changed the dressing and reapplied the gauze he explained that he would be back in two more days to take out the stitches.

As big as the cut appeared, I was not sure I wanted him to take out the stitches.

The doctor and my parent engaged in small talk as they walked together into the hall. I was more interested in the attendant who I now recognized as being from food service who was brining me a mid-day meal. I can't remember what was for lunch I just remember that being the beginning of regular meal service.

Following lunch I welcomed my mid-day meds and just as I was drifting off I encountered another visitor.

He was dressed in business attire rather than the hospital garb that I had become accustomed. As he approached my bed, he offered a handshake, and introduced himself as the orthopedic surgeon who would be working with me.

There's a lot to be said for that handshake. First of all, that handshake signaled to me that for the first time in my life what I thought was going to matter. His firm grip also conveyed this doctor's confidence in his abilities.

He inquired about pain, checked the weight on the traction and he viewed some bandages covering some scrapes and abrasions, soon to become "battle scars."

Dr. Jim explained, in simple terms, the condition of my left femur. This was again news of an injury from an accident I could not relate to. In short, my leg had become pinned behind the driver's seat. When the car hit a tree, the inertia from the collision threw my body forward. The trapped leg was twisted and mashed leaving a six inch section of shattered bone.

There was still uncertainty as to the course of action. He explained that the bone was floating inside the skin and the traction would prevent movement and protect the remaining bone and the muscle surrounding it. He concluded by saying he would be back tomorrow to discuss options with me.

He was middle age-and spoke with a kind, considerate voice, and his voice as with his handshake seemed to communicate assurance that I was in good hands.

The talk between the doctor and my parents seemed to be of a serious nature, but the pain meds were taking over. I remember thinking as I was drifting away, how bad it was going to hurt when they removed that pin running right through the leg just above the knee cap.

The routine for the day was complete with my evening meals. Oh, yes! My final thrill of the day was the introduction of the urinal or the "pee bottle." That's what resulted from drinking all that water. That was just one more adjustment to my trapped existence.

* * * * *

Up to this point only the day-time routine concerned me; up until today there was no difference between day and night. It may have been that morning that I woke up to the physical world, but it was that evening, after I said good night to my parents and after the lights in the room were dimmed that my mind drifted into the spiritual world.

For the first time since this ordeal began I consciously started to reflect on my spiritual journey. I was in awe as I reviewed in my mind my spiritual encounter. I relived, for the first time that "walk through the valley of the shadow of death" and emerging on heaven's door. I was immediately overjoyed. From that evening on my life was more than a personal recovery; it was becoming a walk with God.

That evening I enjoyed another revelation. I was not alone; I was in a hospital ward that at maximum capacity could accommodate four patients. I would share this room with those younger and older and all experiencing uncertainties and a fear of the unknown.

While I had a lot of recovery ahead I couldn't help but feel sorry for those around me, and I would have liked to share my joy but it was all too new, and all I could do was offer sorrow and comfort and prayer. I guess that was a beginning.

CHAPTER 5

WHAT ARE MY OPTIONS?

"Yeah though I walk through the valley of the shadow of death; I will fear no evil."

The remainder of this week would be one of challenges. The emphasis for the week was two-fold. First, to deal with the head injury, and finally to develop a treatment plan for the badly damaged left leg? Both issues would be first addressed on Tuesday.

The neurosurgeon dropped by for a short visit to view the stitches and to change the head wound dressings. My brain specialist was not a part of the St. Johns in house staff but he was instead a distinguished physician on the staff at the Mayo Clinic. He practiced in Springfield one week out of the month and it was my good fortune to have him as a part of my medical team. His Tuesday visit was brief. After a quick exam, we exchanged some humorous small talk and he scurried away, reminding me that he would be back tomorrow to take out the stitches.

After lunch Dr. Jim arrived with my parents. He again offered a confident handshake and moved his chair close to my bed so we could clearly communicate.

He first produced an x-ray that showed the six inches plus of missing bone. He made it absolutely clear that the extent of the damage was severe and that there was a genuine possibility that I could lose my leg.

The fear and panic that shown on my parents' faces made it clear that this extreme consequence had not been a part of any previous discussions.

After allowing time for a reality check, he continued. He explained that there was a treatment that could save the leg. It would involve inserting a pin through both pieces of the bone in my left femur. The two bone ends would be spaced for a gap to allow for the growth of new bone. If bone regeneration was achieved I should heal successfully and I should have a complete recovery.

The procedure was simple but there were risks. First, the bone might not regenerate. Then, there is the possibility that a compromised immune system would not be able to fight off infection around the incision sites. These circumstances would most likely result in amputation. The spacers could slip allowing the bone to grow too little or too much, or the resulting bone could heal with deformities. This was not a routine surgery but it was the only option.

His explanation was clearly stated and left little to the unknown. He asks that we talk this over and have an answer by the next day. He emphasized that the surgery should be done soon to prevent further damage to the remaining bone and tissue.

I honestly believe that we could have answered his question while he was still in the room but neither I nor my parents wanted to discuss it at that moment. I had faith that this surgery was a part of God's plan and that whatever happened, I would be able to deal with it. I was pretty sure that my parents would agree to anything that would save the leg. So the decision was deferred until later. I realized that we would have to have that discussion and be in agreement before morning.

The remainder of Tuesday was routine. I would like to be excited about the food service after all I was getting to fill out my own menu but the BM (Bowel Movement) issue that developed after I started to eat solid food was becoming problematic. The situation was simple if you continue to take in food but fail to release it you will eventually have issues.

This situation could be a physical blockage caused by the accident, or it could be an emotional or trauma related issue, or it could simply be a modesty issue. Regardless of the cause, this predicament stuck around until Wednesday evening. After receiving the ultimatum that an enema could be the only solution, my body relented and nature finally took its course.

Tuesday evening as a family, we addressed the surgery proposal. As I expected, we were all on the same page. Seeing my parents wrestling with this decision forced to mind the consequences of my irresponsible actions. I made my decision based on faith, they made there's based on fear.

In the quiet on Tuesday evening after visitors left and the lights were out, I had another come to Jesus meeting about this surgery. I totally considered all options. I accepted the idea that my life would go on even if I did lose my leg. I knew again that I was in God's hands and I would be able to deal with the results, whatever they might be.

The highlight of Wednesday was the removal of my stitches. The neurologist arrived shortly after breakfast and with quick scissor action he snipped all of the long, black threads.

When I viewed the results, it was still shocking. First of all, there was no hair on my head. This had been a worry of mine. Could hair grow on a scalp that was badly damaged?

That was a foolish worry. It would just take time. Since my body was busy budgeting energy to healing, hair growth might be on down its list.

Another thing I noticed was that in place of the stitches were large indentions in the scalp. The doctor assured me that as the skin tightened, the indentions would fill in.

Before he left he cautioned that when I cough or sneeze it might feel like I was coming apart at the seams. That also would get better as the skin stretched.

The scar was almost scary and with no hair to cover it up, I was wondering what people would think. The doctor comforted my anxiety by saying a good plastic surgeon could close that scar to a thin line and as long as I had hair it would be barely noticeable. Following his comments he dismissed me from his care and he was gone.

I almost forgot the BM resolution. That was a cause for celebration. Cheering and balloons and ice cream were all a part of this major problem resolution. We cheer for even small wonders.

Dr. Jim stopped by early in the day for our decision and then came by after his last surgery to report that the procedure was scheduled for Friday at 7:00 a.m. He promised more time and a complete outline of the event on Thursday.

As this night approached I thanked God for the abilities of the doctors on my recovery team. I also accepted the head scar and all the other visible scars as battle wounds, evidence of that very special day when God and I bonded. They were scars of courage and survival. They were signs that served as personal reminders of the powers of God and the hope of eternal life.

Thursday I was actually looking forward to eating. I had conquered the intake-outtake issues and I knew that beginning at midnight my diet would go back to restricted.

Preparation for surgery was the Thursday theme. In addition to the regular vitals checks, the nurses were busy collecting lab specimens for pre-surgery testing. My midnight body temperature was a little above normal. This created some mild concern but the nurses explained that the lab work would isolate any surgery stopping situations.

When the doctor arrived he did a visual exam of the leg from hip to knee. He checked to see that all of the cuts were healing properly. He scanned for any unnatural swelling.

In regard to the procedure he explained that a stainless steel pin would be inserted in the bone through a small incision in the hip. Next, there would be a long deep incision through the flesh on the thigh. This opening would allow for the pin to be properly spaced through the gap area and so it could be inserted into the lower bone fragment. The incisions would be stitched and the healing would begin immediately. As soon as the anesthetic wore off I was to begin working on muscle development and joint mobility.

Dr. Jim said that final surgery prep would begin in my hospital room about 5:00 a.m. and I would be taken down for surgery about 6:30. He reminded me about no food or drink after midnight. He alerted me that the anesthetist would be in later to discuss his role in the surgery. Before he left he extend that hand for a final handshake and said he would see me in the "OR".

After all of that, my main concern still centered on that pin that was running right through the knee. I was really ready to get rid of it. It was a visual I wanted to erase.

With all of the formalities of the week, we were all ready for an early evening. By 8:00 p.m. my room was clear and it was just me. My parents left with that same anxious look they had since the doctor mentioned the possibility of amputation. I wished they could share the Peace that I was experiencing. They were so close to it. It wasn't long before sleep came. I was awakened briefly, as always, at midnight and remember the nurse taking my large water glass and my pitcher of ice water.

CHAPTER 6

SURGERY DAY

I could tell today was going to be different beginning with my 4:00 a.m. meds and vitals' check. I always woke briefly during med. This morning it was still dark outside but the shadows of hospital light illuminated an image standing at the foot of the bed. In my drowsy state I first thought it was an angel.

A closer look identified the figure as one of the many sisters-of-mercy attached to the hospital to minister to the patient's spiritual needs. With my enhanced relationship with the creator, it was a welcomed sight to see the sisters. Their comforting words were a meaningful compliment to the medical services provided by the hospital. A sister might pay you a visit anytime of the day. You could expect a visit from a hospital chaplain twice a day, once in the morning and once in the evening.

The sister explained that she knew I would be going to surgery soon and ask if we might pray together. While I was working hard on being brave, her calming words brought back my earlier spiritual experience and wrapped me with the assurance that I was in God's hands. That was my real prep for surgery.

The nurses informed me that they would be in and out between now and the scheduled surgery time to complete the necessary pre-surgery preparation. As I expected more blood was drawn and my IV was reinserted in the port established when I was first admitted. That was a good thing. No more poking and probing. Fresh antibiotics were introduced to my system with some additional liquid nutrition. I was already missing breakfast. As a final, unexpected item on the prep agenda, a male nurse shaved me from my waist to my toes and I received a rub down with some kind of antibacterial gel.

My parents arrived about 5:30 followed by the doctor and the anesthesiologist. After a quick review of the procedure, a nurse put some sedation medicine in my IV drip and an orderly removed me from the security of my hospital room. Mom and dad walked by my side as I moved closer to the elevator. My mom held my hand as we rolled down the dark quiet hallway. Just before the elevator doors opened she gave me a kiss on the cheek. My father offered me a pat on the shoulder. The doors closed for the ride down to the lower level surgery rooms.

I was really interested in what was going on and had plans to pay really close attention to this whole surgery experience. As we rolled down the corridor to the operating room I stared at that pin going right through the knee. I focused on that as we entered the OR.

A bright, white, sterile environment greeted the eye and a clean, antiseptic smell caused my nose to wrinkle. The surgery team was outfitted in hospital garb and their faces were covered. I recognized the doctor's voice and linked it to the self-assurance of his handshake. The last voice I remember was a near faint voice explaining that I was to start at one hundred and count backwards. As I began counting I glanced one last time at the pin through the knee. I don't remember ninety-eight.

* * * * *

The room was cold. The lights were still bright, but everything was very foggy. My eyes were having trouble focusing. I heard voices; distant and unfamiliar. It was like I was in a room, but nobody knew I was there. Then, I saw a figure in my face.

A recovery room nurse spoke quietly, "Welcome back," the voice in my space, announced. "The doc's got you all fixed up. As soon as we get you cleaned up you'll be ready to entertain visitors."

It was slowly beginning to make sense. I was in a hospital. I had just under gone surgery. I must be in recovery. I was now focusing and I understood that I was in a room with several other patients, all trying to make sense of the moment.

A couple of orderlies flanked either side of my bed and I was again on the move. Four floors up on the elevator and down the hall; I was again in my room, in my corner spot close to the door. It was my security.

The room was full. I first noticed my mom and dad. Mary and Stan were there as well as Don and Dora Crites. I felt immediate concern with the presence of all of these folks in the same room. There were still a lot of unanswered questions.

Stan announced that he had been dismissed and would be going home today. He stayed close to his mother and had little else to say. Don and Dora were on their way to Branson to visit Donnie. They dropped by to visit my folks on surgery day.

With all that was going on in my life I had thought little of my traveling companions. This immediate gathering made me uneasy. Maybe it was the answer to all of those questions. Maybe I was afraid of the answers. Maybe I was afraid of what random conversation might reveal.

I didn't have to worry long. Mary and Stan expressed their well wishes and left. Don and Dora offered to take mom and dad to lunch. Mom walked with the Crites'. My dad stayed behind but said that he would join them later.

Dad again cautiously reminded me to watch what I said about the accident. I should beware of people inquiring about the particulars of the crash. His voice and body language reflected pain and confusion. He just didn't get it. I didn't know enough about the physical event to carry on a conversation. Then there was the spiritual event that I was not secure enough to talk about. Following his words of caution he joined my mother.

Alone again in the room I noticed several changes. First, I was in a different bed. I could reach the up and down buttons on this one. The little trapeze was still there, but the other hardware associated with the traction had been removed. I felt again, for just a moment, a degree of freedom.

Following the surgery I returned to the heavy pain meds. Not long after my guests departed I drifted off to several hours of deep sleep. When I came too it was evening meal time. The fare was nothing to cheer about. Because of the operation my diet had returned to liquids and soft foods. I was only awake long enough to eat a sampling of the dinner offering and I returned to sleep.

Early evening I had a visit from Dr. Jim. He explained that the surgery had gone well. The stainless steel pin was now holding the leg together. He emphasized that the leg was strong and there was no need for a cast.

He said a therapist would be by to help set up an exercise program. The leg should be used as much as possible. It would be stiff, but as the muscle function returned so would my mobility. He then threw back the sheet and for first time I was able to see my legs, fully extended and unrestrained.

The scabs and scares retold the story of a violent physical event. He also pointed out two taped area, one a large section on my thigh where the pin had been aligned, and the second, a small incision on my hip where the pin was inserted. After close examination I noticed the absence of the pin through my knee. What a relief. The only thing remaining was a well-defined hole on both side of the knee.

The doctor also noted that I would again be on the antibiotics because of the deep, extensive incision to the left femur. As far as pain, he said that as soon as the trauma of the surgery faded so would the need for the heavy doses of narcotic pain killers. That was all for that night.

My skin, which had been a golden brown only a week ago, was now almost the same color as the sheets. My muscle tone which had been taut during tennis season was now limp and lifeless. I, for the first time, was thinking about recovery and about healing.

The night nurse said that today I had been a very good boy. Since dinner was such a disappointment she said I could have ice cream for my nightly snack. Ice cream has a naturally calming, sedative quality. That and my 8:00 p.m. meds were bringing this day to an early end.

Before I closed my eye I was blessed with a visit from one of the sisters. It was the same one that prayed with me earlier. We prayed again and for the first of many times to come, I realized that God had bought me through another battle and was preparing me for future service. I thanked him for that and then entered into a sound and healing sleep.

CHAPTER 7

PREPARING FOR THE FUTURE

The remainder of my hospital stay went by quickly. I was somewhat sedated during the remainder of the week-end following surgery, but beginning on Monday, meds were less and less apart of my routine. There were however changes in my routine. First, without the burden of the traction equipment; I was free to trade in the hospital gowns for pajamas. That provided a whole lot of "get well soon" medicine.

During my stay, I encountered a nasty cough. It was serious enough that I received inhalation therapy involving medicated breathing treatments. My medical team was concerned that since I had been on my back for so long, fluid could be collecting around my lungs creating the possibility of pneumonia. Even though I received treatments until just before I was dismissed, my respiratory system began to improve immediately after I started spending more time sitting up than lying down.

My physical therapist worked out an exercise program that included bending and lifting my legs. I was encouraged to sit on the edge of the bed with my legs dangling free during meals and for comfort from time to time. I was allowed to sit part of my day in a chair. I was allowed to use a wheel-chair, with assistance, to go to and from the bathroom. The wheel chair would eventually be replaced with crutches and this transition all took place in five days. Life was good.

The wheel chair was also my ticket to activities outside the hospital room. My first outside experience was a trip to x-ray. This would be a daily trip and was to check on signs that the bone was beginning to regenerate. After the second day there was evidence that bone growth had begun. This was a positive that we were all looking forward too.

Also, on Monday morning, I was treated to another wheel chair excursion. Nobody really explained where we were headed, but time away from the hospital room was "good times." My morning journey reached its end in a room that smelled like the swimming pool at the YMCA.

The orderly who was pushing me asked if I was ready for a swim. This was a bit of a surprise but it sounded inviting. That pleasant thought was immediately replaced with that anxious feeling that comes with new hospital experiences. A quick scan of the room revealed a huge bowl resembling an above ground swimming pool. It was made of shiny stainless steel and was about five foot deep in the middle. A liquid mist hung on the air.

Also, like most hospital experiences, one has little time to think it over. A therapist took me from the orderly. He traded me a big towel for my pajamas, but he assured me that they would be returned. By now I was in "follow direction mode". This was something that I had no control over and somebody thought it would make me better. I did as instructed and covered up with the towel.

There were questions forming in my mind but most were answered before they became complete thoughts. I next was wheeled to a huge chair that was attached to a long arm. Once I was positioned in the chair they fashioned the towel lining the chair around me like a diaper. I was strapped securely into the chair and I was off. The long arm was lifting me up and over the ledge of the giant stainless bowl. Next, I began to drop into the water. My toes touched the water and as it came up on me it felt nice, like warm bathwater. I continued into the water until I was chest deep.

The first time I had an opportunity to speak, I assured them that I was fine. A gentle wave action began. The treatment lasted about thirty minutes and involved different levels of water motion and a variety of simple water exercises for my legs and knees. When the jets stopped the long arm lifted me up and I was returned to my wheel chair. I was greeted with a number of hot fluffy towels to dry with. I got dressed and was ready to head back to my room.

I had completed my first hydro-therapy treatment. I would receive this treat once daily for the remainder of my stay. It was something I looked forward to.

The doctor made his rounds daily. He checked for mobility of the joints and the muscles especially around the incision site. He carefully interpreted the daily x-rays and when he had conclusive proof of bone regeneration he begin to pitch a dismissal day.

There were two requirements for my dismissal. One, I must be able walk without assistance, with crutches and finally, I would have to be able to control my pain with oral painkillers. As each part of the puzzle began to come together I began to consider how my life would be "after hospital."

When it comes to healing, one should never underestimate the value of connecting to the outside world. As the influence of the pain medication began to diminish, I began to notice more closely the world around me. My little corner of the room was decorated with balloons, and flowers and I had a stack of cards and letters. As I noticed the effort that was being made on my behalf, those feelings of guilt crept back in. This was all so nice, but that didn't change the fact that it was my poor decisions that made this "get well" session necessary.

The weekend after surgery was a busy one. First, my grandparents from Sallisaw, and my brother, Tom were Saturday afternoon visitors. I experienced special feeling of regret when I saw them. I know they were kept at a distance to the situation and that that was wrong. I was glad to see them but my father dictated a brief get well, we love you dialogue and then escorted them away. I became tearful again as they were whisked away and I was so sorry for the circumstances we were all being forced to adjust to.

Later in the day, Donnie Crites joined the patients in our room. He transferred to St. Johns to receive enhanced treatment for fractured vertebrae. He was resting on what looked like an ironing board, and every so often he would be turned. Sometimes he was looking at the ceiling and sometimes he would be staring at the floor.

This whole contraption was the subject of many jokes but it looked terribly uncomfortable. His pleasant, sparkling attitude was an added component to my "get better" cause. With Donnie came Don and Dora. Don was a great cook and kept our ward in the best of treats for the duration of my stay. Donnie's parents were also great company for my parents, especially my father.

That Saturday was the turning point in my recovery. Vicki, the girl I met in marching band two years ago, and my very best friend burst into the room with a brand of joy that could only result in positive ends. She and one of our mutual friends were visiting straight from camp. I had read cards and letters from Vicki but I didn't realize how much I wanted to see her.

Her visit was short and I don't think she was prepared to see me in a hospital bed. We exchanged tears, but that visit was to begin a transition from friendship to a life we would share together. Her personality was uplifting and she became my number one reason to get better.

I continued to receive cards and letters from her throughout my recovery both in the hospital and after I went home. She was the angel at the foot of my bed. She was full of unconditional love for me and my family.

I had other visitors during the week. Relatives paid one last weekend visit before they began their busy work week. I had a few visitors from high school and college but I really didn't expect many as I was in a Springfield hospital, an hour's drive from home. Details of the car crash were sketchy and most of my friends new nothing of the accident.

The visits from the insurance representative were moments of high anxiety. While all of his visits to me were positive, they were constant reminders of the mistakes that initiated this whole chain of events. His presence also seemed to rekindle a flame of indecision and mistrust in my father.

By Tuesday, it was time to get serious about meeting the doctor's objectives for dismissal. He had set a tentative dismissal day for Friday. Beginning with my morning meds I received my pain control medicine by mouth. Also, immediately after my morning swim, I was deposited in the physical therapy area of the hospital for my first walking lesson.

I was greatly deceived about how little I really remembered about walking. My only exercise for that day was to pull myself up between parallel bars, stand up right, and then take a step. This sounded like a trivial waste of time. I was able to use upper body strength to lift my body from the wheel chair, but as it reached the upright position my legs buckled as the blood all rushed from my brain and I passed out.

I awoke in my hospital bed feeling embarrassed and defeated. My therapist visited me in my room and we discussed the necessary steps in my walking rehab. We had a date on Wednesday after my hydro-therapy. I was determined to be successful.

During the day on Tuesday my meds change went unnoticed but when I was still very active at 11:00 p.m., my midnight pain medicine was delivered as an injection. When the doctor visited on Wednesday he cautioned that I would have to be off all injections before I could be released.

Challenges loomed over Wednesday. There were only two days before my scheduled dismissal and I hadn't achieved either of my milestones to freedom. My water treatment that day was not as enjoyable as the others as I had to deal with the walking issue. I must admit the water energized me.

This time when I pulled up on the parallel bars I moved slowly giving my blood a chance to establish an equilibrium thus eliminating the fainting reaction. Once I was stable I cautiously stepped forward. After that first step I took another and then another, one foot in front of the other, and I was at the end of the bars.

There was cheering and I realized that celebrations are for even small things like one step. With this improvement, the therapist scheduled an afternoon session for more practice and the possibility of adding crutches. I also had this notion that if I had more activity, natural sleep would be easier to achieve. Even this short amount of activity had drained most of my energy and I welcomed the security and comfort of my corner suite.

My afternoon walking session went great and I even received instruction on how to use crutches. My assignment was to use my crutches to get out of bed, to use the bathroom, and to take some short assisted walks. In addition to the warning about my meds, the doctor also stressed the need for confidence on crutches as a key to my success in the outside world.

It was difficult at first, but patience was the key. Quick moves and speed were not a part of my immediate future. I took my practice seriously and by evening med, the pill was enough. Even with Donnie in the room, we both quieted and I remember only waking briefly at midnight med time.

By Thursday all the talk was dismissal. What a difference a day made. The doctor's visit was very positive. The x-rays looked good and his opinion was that I should lose the crutches as soon as possible. He felt that I might move to a cane in about five days and on my own as soon as I felt secure.

Only three days ago I passed out just trying to stand. Thursday was almost a celebration. Then there was Donnie. He had been my hospital companion and we shared much, but talk of the accident was minimal. My last night at the hospital was uneventful except for the ice cream late night snack.

Friday I started out in a rush and ended up waiting. I hurried to make sure I had one more water session and I looked forward to receiving tips for success from my therapist. Then it was back to the room to pack.

Lunch came and went and I was waiting. My parents arrived and now we were all waiting. Mid-afternoon the doctor signed my dismissal papers and scheduled my next appointment. A nurse brought by the name of a plastic surgeon and took care of making our first appointment.

The wheel chair guy arrived and we packed up the flowers and cards and letters and we were ready to leave. I wheeled over to Donnie and we visited briefly and we said our goodbyes. That goodbye was to be more significant than I realized.

As I passed through those halls and out into the sunlight I thanked God for my being. I thanked him for the doctors and nurses, for the sisters and the chaplains, and for the therapists. I thanked God for my parents, for my family, for my friends and for my relatives. I thanked Him for the gift of healing and I thanked him for forgiveness. I knew that my life of service lay ahead and I asked God for guidance.

CHAPTER 8

LEAVING SANCTUARY BEHIND

This is the place where I explain why I have spent four chapters in the hospital. After Chapter Three my life should be one of ease and leisure. I have met the Master. What greater thing could happen? When do I start changing lives and making the world a better place? With God as my Commander-in-Chief when do I start defeating evil in the world?

If you remember, as I began to travel back from heaven I immediately felt the purity of the moment fade as perfection slipped back to a flawed and sin filled world. I am no longer in God's House. I am acting in our world; in a world where an absolute knowledge, more than just faith, doesn't assure anything. The reason is mankind; there is always free choice.

Hospital stays are often times of sorrow and suffering. When I was personally delivered by the arms of God, I was filled with Faith and Hope. I was absolutely committed to those assigned to my recovery team. The presence of the sisters and the chaplains helped me develop a solid "Faith Base."

It was in one of my hospital reflection sessions after "lights out" that I realized at the moment of death, when I experience that snapshot of my life, my anxiety was high as I awaited the revelation of all of my earthy sin. My human reaction to their absence was that they had been overlooked. It was like someone hit the delete button and I was re- formatted. A deeper inspection allowed a calm acceptance that my sins were forgiven. I had a clean slate.

Let's take a look at my situation. First, I had been forgiven by God. Even this last indiscretion had been wiped clean. But while we answer ultimately to God, we live in this world. I had unresolved issues with my family, I had unresolved issues with my friends, and I had unresolved issues with the school. While I have complete trust in God, my trust with those I love has been compromised. My current status includes lost opportunities and lost friendships. There are still questions to be answered.

I was nurtured and showered with God's blessings during my hospital stay. When I walked out that door that foundation that I worked so reverently to build during my days of recovery would be immediately challenged. While I conquered victory over death, my next battle, serving my God on earth was to be much more difficult.

CHAPTER 9

FROM DARKNESS TO LIGHT

Sitting in the back-seat of the family car, securely restrained by a seatbelt, was not scary, but as soon as my father pulled the car into traffic I was fighting a panic attack. My go home medication rescued me and I slept until we pulled into my driveway. To see home was a comforting site, but that comfort was short lived.

As I maneuvered my crutches and slowly approached the front door I noticed the curtains were pulled tight and the house looked unoccupied. It in fact had been unoccupied so I guess that was not so strange. As I hobbled through the front door, I entered a dark, cold environment. I was trading my bright, cheerful hospital residence for this cold, dark creepy world of denial.

My father, the trained counselor, was in denial of the whole event. His son had survived a fiery, automobile accident. Even though his son's recovery was an absolute miracle, he was bothered by what people would think. Was his son a teenage drug addict or an alcoholic? How could he counsel other people's children when his own was out of control? Then there were the failing grades, something else the public could use to judge him. He had been harboring all of his frustrations for the past two weeks.

The medication didn't allow any more time for reflection. All of this out of the ordinary, confusing stuff would have to wait. I immediately went to bed and slept the remainder of the day.

When I awoke the next day things were a bit clearer. I had hoped that my earlier appraisal of the home front was clouded by my medicated state. In reality, the symbols of denial were more obvious. As time went on I noticed the absence of the telephone. When the door- bell rang we were not allowed to answer it. The television was seldom in use. My brother was still away. This entire arrangement was to satisfy my father. He seldom left the house himself. Depression was hanging in the air.

Mothers are just different. Mine was very quiet and very accommodating. While she went along with this complete state of withdrawal, that didn't mean she agreed. One afternoon dad left to take care of business. It was the first time I had been alone with mom since the accident. She confided that she was uncomfortable with the way things were being handled.

She recounted that immediately after hearing of the accident he became very withdrawn. He had the phone taken out, and began avoiding people. The crash had left him helpless in a situation that he had no control over.

He was frustrated and angry. She said that he insisted on this new life style because he felt that for my speedy recovery I needed an environment that was quiet and void of outside interference. He also felt that for my emotional stability, I should not have to recount or discuss anything relevant to the accident.

It was a good thing that my father had left us alone because my mother wanted to hear all I could remember about the day of the accident. As I have said many times, there was little I could remember about that day. As we continued to talk I began to understand that it was not so much the physical account that interested my mother.

I began with a tearful apology for all of the hurt and pain that my selfish recklessness had created and I thanked her for being there and loving me even though she had every reason to be angry.

She then revealed the spiritual alert she received. While teaching her kindergarten students her thoughts became cloudy. She visualized an image of me with an angel. The angel was holding me up and I appeared with outstretched arms and an appeal for Help. She said the look on my face was one of helplessness. The vision was real. While the vision was startling it was not frightening. It was just minutes before her principal and a fellow teacher called her out of class and reported to her the accident. She told me that she already knew. She also said that she was not afraid as she received comfort from the angel.

It was now clear that she knew something of my heavenly encounter and I felt relieved to share it with someone. You can always share with your mother. You know she will hear you out without being judgmental. I told the story just as I recounted it in Chapter 3. It felt good to share. We talked it over but didn't reach any kind of decision as to what I should do with the story. We both felt that sharing it with my father in his current state would achieve nothing. For a long time she was the only one I was comfortable to talk with about that miraculous time.

I discussed the snapshot judgment and the forgiveness of sin. I explained the excitement surrounding the absolute revelation of heaven.

It was hard for me to understand why my father and I were so far apart. He had nothing to feel bad about. He wasn't the one who had made a mistake. I was alive. He had nothing to fear. Yet our relationship had been badly damaged and it would take time to repair.

For now all I could do was adapt to this lonely existence, and pray that peace might conquer this skeptical, cynical time in my life.

For a complete week I stayed at home. Dad was in and out and life began to again take on definition. I was beginning to understand my dad's position but continued to pray that he might be able to accept the present and move on. It's so hard to see people you love suffer when Peace is so close.

My first outing came one week after my release from the hospital. It was a trip to refill a prescription. I was able to maneuver pretty well on the crutches but this was the first time I had been out in public.

My head was still bald and my scar was unavoidable. While I really wanted to be out of that house, I wasn't ready to deal with the stares and the somber comments. I wasn't ready to return to the secular world.

I wasn't ready for the stark contrast to my heavenly experience. I now looked at the world differently. I see a world crying out for help.

I'm getting ahead of myself. There's a lot of healing left in my small world. So it's back to the house and back to dealing with my own set of needs.

The next day was Sunday. My first venture in public was an emotional disaster. Mom suggested that we go to church. Dad asked if I thought I could deal with another outing. He reminded me about all of the steps and whether I could handle them with my crutches. He seemed surprised when I said yes. I prayed that this might help break down the wall that separated me from my father and my father from the peace we all deserve.

While it seemed out of character for my father to agree to the church event, I was praying that he might experience the power of God and that this might be the beginning of our healing.

When we arrived at church we were a little late which meant that we didn't have to deal with many people. When I entered the building I could feel God pulling me in, closer and closer. When we reached the doors to the sanctuary I was ready to rush in, but my father deferred that entry and led the way to the elevator that led to the balcony. We made it to God's House, had executed the stair to enter, and now we were sitting in the balcony. This arrangement was again to avoid people and to avoid questions.

From the moment we joined the service, I felt God's presence like never before. I had attended church services since I was a young child, but I had never felt this spiritual connection. The words, the music, the testimony all presented to glorify God. I was so personally involved that I failed to notice the strained looks. Dad's face started to soften. I failed to see the tears that followed. I failed to see my mom hold him close as he began to surrender.

On this particular Sunday the minister announced an altar call. I felt disappointment when I realized that I was far from the Altar, in the balcony. The minister looked to the balcony and as if speaking to me instructed us to come to the stair leading to the balcony. I was up and moving. I knew that God would give me the strength to go all the way. I expected some resistance but the power of the Holy Spirit was guiding

Calvin Cassady

me. When I reached the stairway, it was full all the way to the Alter. I felt assurance that I was a part of a large group who were making this public statement as to their relationship with God. When I looked up I saw both my mother and my father joining with the many who were willingly surrendering their current status in exchange for God's Peace. The time for healing was at hand.

CHAPTER 10

DAMAGE CONTROL

The next ten months were damage control. Nothing was ever said about that Sunday church service, but in the coming days my father began to rise from his spiraling depression. He never talked of the accident. He was putting it behind him.

During the summer there was a trial to determine the amount of liability to be paid. My dad did all he could do to keep me from those proceedings. He said he didn't want me to have to relive the whole scary ordeal and he said he didn't want me to be in a position to have to testify at a trial that involved my friends. This was his only reference to the accident for the rest of the summer. My mother stood by me during this time always providing support and encouragement.

The quiet, uninterrupted home climate continued as my father and I together tried to salvage my education and get it back on track. The dreaded discussion of my failing grades was mostly accepted as a failure to turn in semester projects and failing to take the semester finals. Talk of all the diversions that I previously mentioned were referenced but not charted as a cause for my academic set back. Notification to turn in late work or make up finals came and the deadline passed while my family was still at the hospital. My father was willing to accept those deadlines as a battle we didn't want to fight.

Dad was a counselor, and a very good one. Within days he had outlined a plan that would include several correspondence classes, heavy class schedules during the school year and attending the summer term following my senior year. If I could achieve those goals, I would still earn my degree in three years instead of four.

I first had to apply to the University of Arkansas for special student status and then I had to request that my Joplin College accept credit from an outside institution. Following these formalities I filled out my enrollment papers and waited anxiously to put this plan in motion.

I was getting stronger and by the end of the third week I was walking without assistance. My June doctor's appointment was very positive. The bone growth was solid and the gap was almost closed. The doctor said that if my recovery continued at this rate I could return to normal activities following my July check-up. My dad asked him about traveling. The doctor saw no reason why I couldn't.

Travel plans included a trip to Sallisaw. These plans served multiple purposes. The family would be reunited with my brother and I would have a chance to spend some quality time with my grandparents. This trip would keep me out of reach to any attorneys attempting to subpoena me for the up-coming trial, and finally, it would give me a chance to be outside without the interference of people.

It was a good idea and I truly enjoyed being able to be out of the house. I was able to get some exercise and some sun, and I got to enjoy being with loving, caring family.

Throughout my lonely home recovery, one person continued her campaign to keep me connected. After I got home from the hospital, I received a letter from Vicki almost daily. She was also allowed visiting privileges. During those early weeks she was a constant reminder of the future. It was always a privilege to return her letters. When I was out of town with the family I missed her correspondence, but I would keep her up to date on my activities. Then when I returned home I would have a stack of letters to catch up on. Vicki was slowly working her way into my heart.

When I returned home after the Fourth of July, my books and lessons from the University of Arkansas were waiting. The climate at home was growing more relaxed. I was on minimal medication and with the study materials I was slowly developing a new routine.

The trial was over so that tension was gone. Soon after the trial a representative from the insurance company visited and assured us that all bills, past and future would be paid in full. He said that we would talk about a final settlement after all the hospital and medical bills were paid. That was a heavy load lifted.

It was good having my brother around. In the weeks to come I revealed as much as he wanted to know about the accident and my hospital recovery. I also expressed my sorrow that he had not been better informed. While I was quick to give total credit to God for my recovery, I didn't touch on my unique spiritual blessing.

Having him home also provided some leverage for more outside contacts. Vicki continued to write and would visit when she had time off from her duties at Girl Scout camp. Home was again the center of a loving, active family. Accept for the absence of the phone, we were beginning to function as a normal family. Even with Tom and I whining in unison, dad would not relent on the phone. He promised that it would be in service when school started.

By the end of July, I was nearing completion of one of my classes and was working hard on the second. There were other classes I needed but I could only be enrolled in two at the same time. I also would have to wait until school started to take my finals as they had to be supervised by a college instructor.

My July doctor's visit revealed almost complete bone recovery and as promised I was released to do normal activities; that included work. My hair was also starting to grow back, but the scar was still noticeable. Before the accident I had been employed by the local grocer. While being with my friends at work seemed almost exciting I was not ready to put that kind of stress on the healing bone.

Since summer was winding down and I was ahead on my lessons, my dad proposed another road trip. We traveled to Indiana to visit my aunt and uncle and several cousins. This was one of my mother's sisters and this was a much deserved break for her; she had quietly and caringly held this family together through our biggest challenges.

The farm and caring people provide the perfect recipe for healing. I had visited these relatives many times and I knew it would be the middle of haying season. That would involve all the cousins. I was afraid that I would be left at home.

I found that I could drive a tractor and could go out with the crew daily. My uncle believed in paying for a good days work so our 10 day visit proved to be not only therapeutic, but also added to my cash flow. Did I mention my aunt's cooking was something to look forward to? Perhaps the greatest achievement of this monumental summer was the sense of accomplishment and self-worth that followed that trip to the farm.

When we returned from Indiana it was August. School was staring us all in the face. Mom had things to do in her kindergarten classroom and my dad would soon be involved in enrollment. My brother was in high school. I enrolled for my first semester college classes.

Being an education major your senior semester classes are predetermined. To add another hour to my transcript I enrolled in marching band. Besides class it involved parades and marching at football games. Balancing all of this with work took a bit of magic but when school started it all worked.

As marching season came to an end I was proud to receive an Outstanding Bandsmen Award for my contribution to the college Band. This was especially meaningful because the physical demand of the class challenged my reduced stamina in regard to the healing bone.

In early November, my bone doctor cleared me for six months. He told me that I should think about having the pin removed at some point as it had served its purpose. He said its prolonged presence could become problematic as it could be a place where arthritis could begin. We agreed to evaluate that situation in six months.

Also in November I had my consult with the plastic surgeon. He came highly recommended and I had to wait a long time for this appointment. He immediately noticed that I now had a full head of hair. That was a good thing because looking at my father he said balding did not seem to run in the family. He said that my hair would cover the scar but he insisted that it would be hardly noticeable when he was finished.

He reviewed the procedure. It would be a long surgery lasting about seven hours. It was also a surgery that would be done with me partially awake. I must admit that that seemed a bit daunting. He said the first available date for surgery would be in March. It could be done during spring break and I would not have to miss any student teaching. We scheduled it.

While the band class was time consuming and was physically taxing, it kept me in touch with Vicki. Her constant interest in my recovery had brought us closer together, and we were beginning to share and find out we had much in common.

Our relationship continued to grow throughout my senior year. She was always willing to wait on me when I fell behind and provided encouragement when I would easily tire or find some tasks physically challenging. We were also taking part in family holidays. We enjoyed family gatherings at Thanksgiving and looked forward to spending Christmas together.

As Christmas drew near and the semester came to a close. Student teaching assignments were posted. I was assigned to teach sixth grade at a rural elementary school, a wing school of a neighboring school district. I successfully completed all of my scheduled classes and I received passing grades on my correspondence courses. I was not completely caught up, but I was getting close.

The student teaching semester was six weeks of prescribed course work. The remainder of the semester was spent in the classroom teaching. That allowed no room or time for additional classes. I worked at the grocery store until Spring Break. When practice teaching started college students were not allowed to have a job.

My six weeks of core classes went by quickly. During this time I had an opportunity to visit my student teaching classroom and meet my cooperating teacher. It was good to know that I had a classroom and students who would be depending on me to provide a part of their education.

My excitement for student teaching was tempered with thoughts of the surgery on my forehead. I knew that I would have most of my hair shaved and I remembered how long it took to grow back. I brushed back my hair to reveal the wide jagged scare. It was still scary. For the first time since the accident I had doubts. I was starting to obsess.

It took just a few moments of quiet reflection to realize that when problems are beyond you, God is just a prayer away. Later that evening I received a phone call from Don Crites Sr. He informed me that his wife's hair stylist had a wig fashioned like my hair and I could use it as I pleased.

What a relief! There was a back-up plan. I could now go into this surgery with confidence.

In early March I reported to the outpatient surgery center in Springfield, Missouri, for my scheduled forehead procedure. Although I received much reassurance, the idea of seven hour of surgery was worrisome. After a sedative, my only instructions were to let the doctor know when I felt the steel of the needle. If I let the doctor know then, I wouldn't feel the pain of my next shot. My eyes were covered and I was only semi-conscious.

I must have been able to feel the steel because I never felt the pain. When he completed his needle work, he held a mirror before me. The jagged edges of the original scar were gone. The scar was softened with hundreds of tiny small stitches that closed the remains of nasty head laceration. My hair was short, but not shaved.

My parents, once again, poured me into the back seat of the car for the ride home. At home it was off to bed and it was morning before I had another thought about it.

Shortly after beginning my student teaching I decided to loose the hair piece. This revealed my very short hair and bandages covering the stitches. As you can guess, my students were full of questions. Those questions became an invitation to share my story for the first time. It was easy to share with young people. They listened and they ask questions and they believed.

Wasn't talking about God in a public school forbidden? I was only a teacher in training. Wasn't that a pretty bold move?

Maybe, but not a single class that I would have in the future missed that testimony.

Student teaching was the defining moment of my college years. It provided proof that I was born to teach. It also afforded me the opportunities to listen and learn, understand and care, and to identify and solve problems. I couldn't wait to get my own classroom.

My wait was short lived. Even before my student teaching experience ended, I was offered a contract to teach fifth grade at the same building for the next school year.

So much had happened on my spiritual journey since this time last year. When I look back I saw evidence of God's work at every stop along the way. I felt almost selfish. While God's presence was evident in my life, it seemed that it was only to hold me up. I had spent a whole year just to get back to where I was. The difference is that this year was lived for God. I stumbled a view times, but I always found my way back.

With a strong body and with a strong faith I was ready to take the next step along my spiritual path.

CHAPTER 11

COLLEGE TO THE CLASSROOM

That last year of college was a ride, but God held on to me tight. Those months following the accident and the transition back to school were rough, but I began to accept help. I learned that when times get rough God is only a prayer away.

The tempo of life didn't slow down during those summer months. While I had finished my student teaching semester, I still had course work to complete before I could receive my diploma. I had signed a contract to teach for the fall semester but the contract would only be valid if I had a teaching certificate. There was a lot riding on that summer term.

Going to class, and going to work took up most of my time that summer. I looked forward to being with Vicki on her time off. We still wrote to each other because our time during the week was minimal. Summer school and camp both were completed by the end of July.

Summer graduation was in August. When I received my diploma, I had completed my obligation to the college. That also allowed for me to receive my teaching certificate fulfilling all things necessary to accept the teaching position. I had completed my educational goal to complete college in three years.

My dad said that joining the work force a year early would put me ahead of all of my classmates and would put me in line to retire sooner. Sometimes I think that my father was too practical.

Graduation is not all that happened that August. Immediately following graduation Vicki and I started looking at engagement rings and before the end of the month we announced our engagement. We were planning a December wedding. Not much time for celebrating. Vicki had to get ready for her senior semester and I was getting ready for my first real class.

* * * * *

The nation is the early 70's was struggling in the post-Vietnam era. The economy was drifting into recession. Unemployment was on the rise and many parents were without work. Also entitlements were becoming a fact of life. For the first time in American history some adults felt they would be better off on welfare than working.

My first teaching assignment was in a small farming community. The majority of the families had an agricultural background but many had given up on the farm to work in blue collar jobs in nearby towns and cities. With the recession, many were unemployed. Entitlement programs and the remnant of the "ME" culture influenced many households. Family values were undergoing change. A conflict developed between a generation of proud farmers and business owners and those seeking entitlements. It was a matter of what one could get in entitlements as opposed to what one could earn

Students during my early years of teaching were products of the "ME" culture. Parents were deeply absorbed in their own needs. Also, there were many children from single parent families or being raised by grandparents. Some families were victims of the war. Some fathers were serving, and some lost their lives and never returned. Other children were love children products of the 'flower child" movement. All of these factors made American classrooms very diverse.

While the people of this community supported their children and teachers at the neighborhood school, they were angry with the school district. The source of their discontent was a decision to close the community high school is an act of reorganization. That meant they had been forced to give up the autonomy of the community school.

Grumblings about consolidation and reorganization made good talk at the barbers and the beauty shop. Parents agreed, however, that they wanted a good education for their children. Also most parents continued to display strong religious beliefs. So the table was set, the challenges were recognized.

Time to get to work!

Given the variables of the group my first task was to create the correct learning environment. It must be a place that was safe and secure. I wanted my classroom to be "the place to be" in the school. I wanted students to want to be there and no place else. It must be a sanctuary of stability and of hope. God's presence was as necessary in that place as in any church.

My students that first year were mostly boys. They were active, energetic youngsters. Children from this era were entering school as "blank slates." They were desperate to find an identity. Most were starved for attention and wanted to be loved. Many were looking for direction and were ready to follow. My mom's loving, caring demeanor and my father's practical side gave me some additional preparation to face the challenges these youngsters offered.

I needed little introduction on that first day of school. Most of my students had a connection to someone in the class I student taught. They had heard all about me and my story. What a first day of school. My spiritual story set the stage for a great sharing session. This was the beginning of a career of sharing. My presentation would never again have a first day impact like it did that day.

School that year became one episode after another. While most days would leave you exhausted, the feeling of accomplishment and success made it all worthwhile.

At home, the wedding plans continued. We would be married in December at the local Episcopal Church. The combination of that first year of teaching, and getting ready for a wedding, made for a very busy time. In retrospect, this was a time for one of God's subtle interventions.

As Thanksgiving passed, and the season changed to winter, all school activities centered on Christmas. Historically, at this time Christmas was still allowed to be celebrated in school. I took it on myself to produce my first Christmas Program. I wrote the script myself and it involved every student in the school.

Inclement weather forced the evening program to be moved to the morning before our dismissal for break. Despite the change it was still well attended. The program gave students a chance to participate in their Christian beliefs. It gave parents an opportunity to see their children perform and to feel good about them.

While politics change, I proudly produced a Christmas Program, with God at its center for the next 20+ years. God and Country were the two things that my musical programs always included.

College prepares one to present the information to the youngster. You go into the classroom with confidence in your abilities to teach stuff. It only took one day in the classroom for me to realize that the job I had been called to do was way more than teaching stuff. I knew that these young people offered me the opportunity to be that role model that many needed. I called on a higher power for confidence in that area.

I became deeply involved in their lives and their families. I prayed daily that I would lead them in the proper direction, one of faith, hope, and success. I realized my biggest failure would be to lead them the wrong way. These were the standards I established for myself and that I strived to attain for my entire career in education

* * * * *

On December 23, 1972 God gave me my greatest earthly gift when he blessed my marriage to Vicki Jo Wilson. Vicki came into my life at its darkest point. She was my support when my future was uncertain. She waited for me when I lagged behind, and she was there to catch me if I fell. My life has been so enriched by our relationship. I feel that we were truly made to be together.

* * * * *

The remainder of that year was a combination of setting up housekeeping and experiencing the lessons of the classroom. The months that followed began a lifetime of sharing. Vicki was also in the classroom completing her students teaching assignment. We began immediately to balance the problems of teaching with the problems of life. In many instances, it was hard to separate the two.

Trying to help a young person develop a belief system was one of my major goals for that first year. They needed to decide who they were. Hopefully, I could mold that image in a positive direction but I learned, that it was not always possible. I also tried to make the parents active players in the education of there children. In some cases we were breaking the "ME" mold and in some cases that was too much to ask in a household.

Conferences were a chance to make that home school connection. In some cases I conducted these school progress visits at the child's home. While some parents looked at this as an invasion; most students saw it as an act of caring for them.

While it is easy to make school about scores, sometimes great successes are buried beneath numbers and per cents. I had to find those students' successes. Parents need to hear those success stories as their children are their greatest investment.

What about failure? Identify it for what it is. Learn from your mistakes and make the necessary improvements. I was a firm believer in children experiencing failure. Failure feels bad. Many times if a student can do things to prevent that feeling of failure, they will be able to self-correct. My role is to help them experience life. That includes happy days, and sad days; good days and bad days, and success and failure. One lesson I wanted to make sure everyone experienced is that we can all be survivors if you'll let God help. That was an offer that I always made.

I prepared for that first year, and I learned a lot. One thing I wasn't ready for was the end of that year. I had planted a lot of ideas and I felt that I had set some kids on the right road but then, just when you think you are on top, the year ends. All that listening, all that sharing, and all that guidance, then you send them back to their parents . . . and then another teacher.

Bridging The Gap

The end of that first year was more of a letdown then most would be. I was being transferred into town. I was leaving all of my connections behind. I would have to start all over again with new students, new teachers, and new co-workers. Do you get the impression that I was just a bit disappointed?

My next conversation with God went something like this. "I listened to what you told me. I did the best I could. I thought I was doing a Great job. Now, this! Why?

I was in one of my not too patient moods and a couple of months passed before I got my questions answered. There was a first grade position opening at my current school. There was a sixth grade position opening in one of the town schools. By transferring to town Vicki could take that first grade position. This was another chance to celebrate; another reason to give thanks.

That following fall we launched a lifetime career in education together.

CHAPTER 12

LEANING ON FAITH

I introduced my spiritual journey in a Christian setting about the same time I began my teaching career. I started attending the Episcopal Church with my wife the year before we were married. Prior to that time I was a Methodist. I became a Sunday school teacher a year later.

My first assignment with the church was to teach the high school class. I took over this class because there was a vacancy that seemed very difficult to fill. It took only one class session to make me realize that the previous teacher was very much liked and his departure was not sitting well with his students. Many, being able to drive themselves, refused to attend those early classes. As the weeks passed I gained an understanding that church politics and a disagreement between the parish priest and the teacher resulted in his resignation.

I allowed some time for the class attendance to stabilize. Then one Sunday morning I slicked back my hair revealing the conspicuous scar and waited. I always opened my church school lesson with a time to share. It wasn't long until there were inquiries about the scar. I introduced my testimony as a story of angels, of heaven and of miracles. That was all it took. I shared that day just as it happened. They listened attentively.

Bridging The Gap

There were a few questions. That opened channels of major sharing. I reached out to that group that Sunday morning and that session was the catalyst for eleven years of Christian growth.

My philosophy was to provide a forum for young people to discuss what was on their minds and relate it back to God. I branded myself a survivor and explained that in God's world we could all be survivors. Growing up today is full of challenges. I put myself out there. I was available, and they came.

The politics of the church didn't necessarily change. There was still a widening gap between the congregation and the priest. This was something I just had to work through. Things would not change for several years.

Because of my success with the high school students, it wasn't long before the middle school kids joined the mix and I also became the youth group director. My wife and I were full of energy and we had no kids of our own, so it was an OK situation. Later that year I became the director of Christian Education.

This elevation in position placed me right in the middle of the church squabble over the need for a new rector. I could deal with the children but dealing with opposing forces in regard to the rector was a new challenge. I began to become disheartened. One of the major obstacles in the church was a lack of concern and lack of funding for the young people. The numbers were growing in all areas of the youth ministry, but that part of the church was on the back burner.

I was so frustrated after an especially disappointing Sunday that I was not only considering resigning from my position but I was considering changing churches. By this time we had added two girls to our family and I didn't want to raise my children in a church that didn't support young people.

This situation certainly was one requiring prayer. My prayer was that God might give me a plan. Should I keep my church membership? Should I keep my church position? As I began to settle in my thinking I considered the road we as parents of church children had traveled together. I decided that there was too much to lose. God has shown me in the past that he doesn't always answer your requests in your time. My wife and I enjoyed the church doctrine. We would wait and see what would happen.

Within a month, the church announced the search for an assistant priest. His emphasis would be on Christian education. This was the church administration's way of postponing a decision on the current rector. I was on the selection committee and we soon issued a call to a young priest to assist the rector and oversee the youth activities. What a welcomed addition. I remained in charge of the church school and continued to teach my high school class. The new hire assisted with all phases of youth activities and became a youth group sponsor. I liked this addition and our youth attendance continued to grow. A parent's group was formed to deal with church school issues. While the congregation wrestled with the issue of the church rector, I continued my quest to strengthen the ties with our church school families.

The young assistance's time with the parish was short lived. While he enjoyed the opportunity to work with the children of the parish, the political tension forced him to look elsewhere and before long he was announcing his resignation. We had worked together as a team and in our short time together he taught me much about the ways of the church. He strengthened my faith and empowered me to be more of a church leader.

In the next few years to follow, I worked on overhauling belief systems. Teenagers seem to want to challenge the status quo. My class was a place where we could recognize God in action. It was alright. Can you tell me where you saw God this week? How did God impact your life this week? How did God help you solve your problems? How about God and your friends?

To show the importance of this group, I moved my class downstairs to St. Margaret Lounge, a space reserved for only important functions. We were meeting with only walls separating us from the adult group. We functioned strictly behind "closed doors." While are conversations were quite serious, the mood was usually light, encouraging participation and the equality of all.

Where else could a teenager exist in this kind of atmosphere? Where else did their thoughts matter? Did this class solve the problems of the world?

Probably not!

Did this class make growing up easier?

Probably not!

Did the class renew the belief system of teenagers? Did it make them participants in a spiritual life?

That was the plan.

My early years were spent talking with young people. It was easy because they were a lot more trusting and accepting. It was not until several years later that I truly understood how seriously they accepted my story. They were once young and accepting; they are now older and believers.

While I was conducting spiritual training behind closed doors, the politics of the church continued to be bitter. The issue, in regard to a new priest, was tearing the parish apart. Through this bitter period, I was referred to by those in my class as "Father Cassady." The parishioners tagged me as the shepherd and the Sunday school kids were the sheep of my pasture. I don't think I have ever felt more honored.

When the politics of the church reached the boiling point we began to hear talk of retirement and the call for a new priest. When the new priest arrived, he was supplemented by two assistants. My duties were scaled back and the title Father disappeared.

The new priest looked on my story as opportunistic and assured me that the whole experience was drug induced.

The following summer I was replaced without cause. I was probably just a victim of the old administration but I will always believe that the new "Father" had trouble with the idea of regular people having that kind of a religious experience.

For the immediate future I was crushed.

The next February my mother was killed in a car crash and I needed to devote full attention to my personal healing and the healing of my family.

God has a way of getting you where you need to be.

The flip side of this story is that later in the "new Father's" ministry, he had his own "vision." It was such a powerful experience that it took a long time for him to accept it for what it was. His "spiritual event" propelled him to a Bishop's position near his hometown. Just another example of how clergy experiences are received.

The idea of miracles is close to me because I am a miracle, we are all miracles at birth, and my survival is a human miracle; my story is a spiritual miracle. I will continue to tell my story in hopes that it can help others along their spiritual journey.

I continue to serve the church when needed. I even took care of the church school again for a time when the next "new priest" came. I am also proud to say that my older daughter, Rebecca, is currently the director of youth programs, ensuring that my grandchildren will receive a proper Christian background.

CHAPTER 13

FRAGILE! HANDLE WITH CARE!

It's been twenty-two years since I sat in the early morning hours at the hospital and listened to the surgeon explain to our family that the damage to mom's liver was too severe to repair. There was nothing more they could do. She died minutes later from injuries she had sustained in a car accident the previous evening.

This story began on a Friday in mid-February. It was two days after Valentine's Day. Today was Drama Day at school, and my students had prepared and acted out scenes from Beowulf. I was very proud of the students as this project engaged each one of them.

As I left school that day I saw the lights were still on in Connie's room. She was my daughter's gifted teacher and we often visited and shared ideas. I dropped in to visit briefly about my drama activity. As we were leaving we found ourselves in a serious discussion. Our words focused our loved ones and about suffering and dying.

Walking out the door I commented, "When it's my mom's time, I want her passing to be quick and with little or no suffering."

We said our good-byes and I started for home to begin a busy evening.

After a quick dinner I left my house to participate in a recreational basketball league. Following the game I headed to the church. I was practicing with a group for the talent show scheduled for Sunday. This situation was awkward as this was my first real activity with the church since I had been asked to resign from my position as the youth minister.

When I arrived at the church, I barely got inside and someone relayed the message that I was to go immediately to the hospital. My mom and dad had been involved in an automobile accident. My dad was not admitted but mom was in the emergency trauma center and her condition was not known. Vicki was already at the hospital.

As I left the church I tried to remain calm. I kept thinking in my mind, "With all that modern medicine has to offer; I'm sure they can fix whatever is wrong."

When I arrived at the hospital I hurried to the emergency room waiting area expecting to see family. I saw no one. I ask at the information desk and a polite volunteer led me to a "quiet room" located in the corner of the lobby.

When I opened the door emotions overflowed into the hall. I heard sniffling and sobbing. Vicki and my sister-in-law Kathi were in the room with my dad.

I focused on my dad. His complexion was ash grey and the expression on his face revealed fear and guilt. His eyes were bruised and swollen and his face had scratches and cuts. His gaze was fixed. I turned my attention to my wife. Tears also stained her face.

Before I could speak, a nurse who knew our family asked to speak to me. We talked outside the room. She told me that they were taking my mom to surgery. I could walk along if I wanted. I followed. I walked the long hallway from the trauma center to the operating rooms. Mom looked peaceful but her head was wrapped and the nurse reported that my mother had suffered head trauma in the accident. She said the immediate worry was internal bleeding possibly from the liver.

The nurse's final words to me before mom was pushed into the operating room area were "I wanted to make sure you had the opportunity to see her while she was still alive. Her injuries are very serious."

As defining as those words were, my faith was still telling me that doctors were miracle workers and even with her serious injuries she would make it. I knew it was possible. I had made it.

The nurse walked with me back to the quiet room. By now my brother had arrived. He just missed getting to take that walk with mom. Vicki joined me. The nurse explained to us that mom was in surgery and that we should move to the surgery waiting area. I walked with my dad and Vicki walked with me. My brother Tom and his wife followed as we relocated to another area of the hospital.

The long night began. The accident happened a little after seven in the evening. Vicki received a call from Marilyn, mom and dad's neighbor. She witnessed the accident. She saw mom and she felt her injuries were serious. She was a nurse. She inquired of the EMT's as to which hospital mom would be going. She then called Vicki. Vicki called the church.

When it comes to accidents, in our family, the details are always sketchy. Apparently this one occurred when dad made a left turn off of a busy four-lane roadway onto the street where our family home was located. It was right at dusk and he failed to see a car suddenly change lanes. The on-coming car collided with dad's car on the passenger side striking my mother.

My father had never been the driver in an accident. Those were the only details available to us at that time. A police officer took my dad's statement before I arrived. In my dad's mind this accident was his fault.

It was now about 9:15 p.m. The first time the surgeon visited with us he reported that when they open my mom, her liver was badly damaged. It was bleeding out-of-control and the primary objective, was to stop the bleeding.

There was a shortage of her blood type and an emergency carrier was on his way from Springfield.

Mom had other injuries, but until they stopped the bleeding, nothing else could be done. Her condition was extremely critical and she would be lucky if she survived. After that discouraging news the doctor asked that we remain in the waiting room. He would let us know if her condition changed.

Again, the message was clear. The forewarning was there. Our family, however, remained optimistic. My dad and my brother continued to reference my miraculous recovery as reason for hope. We continued to pray.

Hours passed. About midnight a nurse reported that her condition was about the same. They had received the blood but the hemorrhaging of the liver continued.

I felt trapped. My anxiety level was rising. I had to get out of that room. Vicki got up to go with me, but she stayed. I wanted to be alone. I was close to an emotional break-down. My thoughts were reeling out of control.

"It's not fair," I wanted to scream! "My mother is dying. Nobody is doing anything about it. Where's God now?'

My instinct guided me into the hospital chapel. God was regaining control. I may have been the only one there. I hope so. I didn't want anyone to see me like that. I collapsed in the pew. It was quiet and it was peaceful. I kneeled; I prayed. By now I was praying for an answer. I heard what the doctor was saying. I prayed for strength; I prayed for a resolution. I sit back in the chapel pew in meditation.

In the calm serenity of that spiritual place God spoke to me. Like before he spoke to my heart. He comforted me with a reminder that my mother's mission was complete.

Selfishness took control for a brief time, but through guided thought God made me realize that her situation was much different than mine. If Mom was offered the gift of eternity, why wouldn't she take it? Why shouldn't she have it? She was a model Christian who was always giving to others. Her life was a life of sacrifice. I knew at that instance that my mother was "heavenly bound."

My family was in a period of preparation. They were not yet strong enough to deal with this great loss. I again kneeled. My prayer was different. "Help me to transition my family from a position of life with us on earth to an acceptance of an eternity in Heaven with God?

God remained quiet on that issue.

I dried the tears that overflowed onto my cheeks and left the chapel. I found myself wandering far from the surgery waiting room. When I began to again focus I was standing in front of the windows at the hospital nursery. God was already softening my loss. He was reminding me that there was a time for everything. Death is the inverse of the miracle of birth. I felt a resurgence of energy and I knew that I had to go back to the waiting area and try to begin this transition

I returned to the same sober tear stained faces. My father immediately embraced me and reminded me again that God had allowed me to live on and he would allow mom to live on. His grip on me was the grip I felt in that hospital ICU unit so many years ago when he declared, "You made it!"

"She will make it," he sobbed.

I fought back tears and tried to speak. This was not going to be easy. My voice was soft and my delivery was hoarse. I was fighting off grief. I remembered the newborns in the nursery and I thought about the miracle of life. Wasn't death also a miracle?

I tried to explain that God sent me back with a mission. I was young and I felt the need to serve. After a long pause I reminded my family of mom's long life of service. Things were different for her. I tried to explain that while giving her up was going to be painful; depriving her of God's gift of eternal life was selfish.

That's what I wanted to say, but I couldn't say those things with meaning. Human nature had a grip on me and I was turning away from God. It was so easy. I'm not sure if I had served any purpose.

I offered prayer, "May God's will be done? May we understand His will? May God give us the wisdom to accept His will, and the courage to live with it?"

I did a horrible job. My family thought I was just giving up. They may even have spoken words of anger.

I realized for the first time that Dad was referencing things that I had never discussed with him. He knew about my journey and that special gift God had shared. Mom must have shared that information with him.

The next update was the beginning of the end. The doctor reported that they were not able to stop the bleeding and that her systems were beginning to shut down. His team had done all they could do but she was just not responding, she fought hard, but she just couldn't make it.

The priest asked if we wanted him to deliver the office of last rites. I accepted his offer. None of us were Catholic but we were all Christians. In the Episcopal Church we recognized the office of last rites. We gathered around her bed and the priest blessed her with Holy Water and prepared her for the spiritual journey. Vicki and I were in the room with her when the monitor straight lined and she breathed her last. I kissed her on the cheek and left her body to the hospital personnel.

We were allowed in for a final look after they unhooked her from all the machines. By then she was no longer mom. Her spirit had passed. Inwardly I wanted to rejoice for her victory. Outwardly, it was hard to let go. I hurt. I was lonely. I was still wrestling with faith.

What now?

The hospital chaplain directed us to a family quiet room adjoining the waiting area. He said we could stay as long as we needed.

Dad was absolutely devastated. He sat and sobbed. He was filled with guilt. He continued to moan that it was his fault. There were things he would need to do and papers he would need to sign. I stayed with him.

Kathi and Tom stayed until they regained their composure. Kathi and mom had a special relationship and mom's passing was a major trauma for her. Tom was clearly moved but he showed little outward emotion. We agreed to all meet at Dad's house when we were able.

Vicki was an emotional wreck, but I think she was the strongest of us all during this time of transition. To her, mom was more than a mother-in law, they were close friends. Mom treated her like she was the daughter she never had. Her death was a tremendous loss. She wanted to stay with me but she knew that there were people that needed to be notified. She took her address book and the chaplain led her to a quiet office where she could deliver the news of my mom's passing.

* * * * *

To: Faculty, Staff, Students and Friends

Saturday, my mother, my best friend and cheerleader, died suddenly from injuries she received in a traffic accident on Friday evening. I ask for your thought and your prayer during this difficult time. I am in a very fragile state and ask to be handled with care.

That was the note I left for coworkers and students at my school.

When we reach the point of surrender, God will always be there. We grieve, we adjust, and we move on. That takes all of our conscious energy. God will carry those who are suffering. He provided us with strength for the days to come.

Maybe the hardest part of this transition period was explaining mom's passing to our girls. They were middle school age and had been brought up with a good church background. I knew how hard this loss was for me to accept. Mom was their hero. How would they deal with it?

Sarah the youngest was openly devastated. I remember her crying uncontrollably during the service. She sobbed and kept repeating, "Grandma Betty is gone. Now, I only have one grandmother left."

Rebecca, the oldest, was more serious. Her response was not outgoing like Sarah's. Her sorrowful comment, "Why did Grandma Betty have to die." Her normal care free demeanor was replaced with periods of anger. It seemed the day she received the news of mom's death, was the day she forgot how to smile.

Neither of the girls viewed mom's body. Because of the head trauma she looked puffy and swollen; Vicki and I wanted the girls to remember Grandma Betty in a happy setting. While we did not discourage them from viewing her body; if they requested to, we would have allowed it. I tried to comfort them with the assurance that what made mom their Grandma Betty was no longer with us, but had passed with her spirit to heaven. They accepted that explanation but that didn't eliminate the hurt associated with the sudden loss.

The funeral director wouldn't let me view mom until Kathi and Vicki agreed that we, me, my brother and dad, could accept her. Because of the face and head distortion we opted out of a public visitation and the casket remained closed. It was only opened for family and briefly at the church after the service. We hosted a visitation at my family's home and we entertained a steady stream of visitors through-out the period from Saturday afternoon to the service time on Monday.

My wife and my sister-in-law displayed emotions similar to my oldest daughter. Their moods would swing from extreme grief to extreme bitterness. They were openly angry with my father and also stated anger with God. I can understand these emotions and maybe it helped them heal. To me it presented more roadblocks to an already treacherous path.

My father's disposition remained unchanged. He was still accepting full blame for mom's death. His position only fueled Vicki and Kathi's bitterness about the whole situation.

Mom died early on a Saturday morning. Her funeral was planned for the coming Monday. That required quick planning. Monday was President's Day. School would not be in session. This would allow her students, their parents, and her co-workers an opportunity to attend her funeral. With the varying states of emotions planning this special event seemed impossible. God's strength and love bound us together and provided us the guidance to carry out the necessities for the service.

Her eulogy for the newspaper and for the funeral service was composed from a collection of documents she had bound together with a rubber band and left on a shelf in the den at the house. We found a collection of pictures on the same shelf. The items in the collection were even arranged in chronological order.

For her final resting place Vicki and I suggested a well shaded lot at a local cemetery. The site faced the east and was across the street from Wal-Mart, her favorite place to shop. One thing mom really enjoyed was shopping. It was only fitting that during the service at the cemetery, red-light specials could be clearly heard. It seemed at the time to be a fitting memorial for one who lived for a bargain.

When we gathered at the house after the funeral it was a time for retreat, a time to comfort each other, a time to begin the process of closure; but not quite yet!

I was blind-sided by the announcement from an elder in mom's family that none of the Native American burial rituals were observed.

Mom was the first of the Winnie clan to die and nobody had notified us of the need for these rituals. There would have been no objection to the inclusion of the rituals. They violated none of my Christian beliefs. It was just too late. All this accomplished was some added sorrow for those that were responsible for planning her services.

In the days ahead Dad was somewhat vindicated when a witness came forward and told police that the car that hit my parents had switched lanes suddenly and had no lights. As quickly as it all happened it was wrong for Dad to feel so guilty. While he cried a tear of relief when he heard the news, he has never really been able to let go, and in a sense, I suffered the loss of both of my parents on that cold week-end in February.

* * * * *

Twenty-two years later I'm still fragile. I can't shake the grief. It usually starts around Valentine's Day and lasts until President's Day, the day of mom's funeral.

Last year Wil, my youngest grandson, had a program in February. While I was sitting in the bleachers waiting for the music, it seemed that mom should be sitting next to me preparing to enjoy the show. Cal, the older grandson, would be sitting on her lap reading the book he had purchased at the book fair. She would be so proud.

Just for a moment I was again consumed with selfishness.

"It's not fair!" She should be here with us."

I'm almost ashamed. I know where she is. I know she is enjoying us, the grandkids, and all the activities of our lives, just from a different vantage point.

There's just too much hurt in February. While I want it to go away, I'm afraid that if I stop grieving I might start forgetting my mother, my best friend and cheerleader. I still need to be handled with care.

CHAPTER 14

STORIES FROM THE CLASSROOM

My biggest influence on students came about in the classroom addressing problems that were interfering with their learning or their self-image. I believe that if a child is dealing with numerous issues outside of school he is not ready to learn, and he will quickly become a candidate for failure.

I prayed daily. I asked God to allow me to do my best, that I might be alert to situations that might need attention, that I would never lead children in the wrong direction, and that I would always remember that God is beside me in times of need.

While I was settling into my new school, God wasted no time in providing me with challenges. Two youngsters were quickly identified as in need of some courage and confidence.

* * * * *

It wasn't long into the school year that I became acquainted with Michael. Michael was a tall slender sixth grader a little bigger than other boys in the room. He had blonde hair fashioned in a Dutch boy style.

He was very interactive and a social magnet for the girls in the class. His school records reported him to be a year older than his classmates. Academically he was failing everything that had to do with reading. In the areas of math and numbers, he was able to get by. As the problems became more and more related to reading and problem solving, his math skills were overshadowed by his weakness in reading.

Being right out of college he seemed to me to be a textbook version of a severely dyslexic student. At this time in educational history that disability was seldom diagnosed and teaching strategies were just beginning to be developed. It was not surprising that he was failing. Because of his passive demeanor and his cheerful personality, he was a perfect subject for social promotion.

You'd think that someone with that much going against him would be bitter and angry about his situation. Despite it all he had good attendance and he seemed to enjoy school. He had never really approached the idea of being a success in school.

Daily prayer led me to research on the subject of dyslexic youngsters and what was known about teaching strategies. I also saw the need to enlist his student support system, which was very loyal. Before long he was learning. He was actually performing as a student. I also quickly discovered that when he could hear or see the information, he had great retention. Oral tests and projects that he designed allowed him an opportunity to display his knowledge. When one succeeds, failure becomes unacceptable.

Outside of school you would see Michael roaming the neighborhood, but he didn't participate in after school activities with the other boys in his class. They asked him to play basketball but he just shook his head, no. When I asked him why a big athletic looking guy like him didn't want to participate with his classmates, he sheepishly replied that he was needed at home.

Michael was being raised by an elderly grandmother along with several other grandchildren including his sister. He had a missing mother, whatever that means. He realized the sacrifice his grandmother was making for her family and felt he was needed to help out. Jenny, the grandmother, was proud to provide a home to the children of her family that were in need.

She was trying to do all of this on a pension. Even with the social security she received for the children she cared for, money was tight.

Being elderly, Jenny suffered ill health and would on occasion be hospitalized. Michael expressed to me his fear that she would die. He took a lot of the responsibility in running the household, much more than should be expected of a 12 year old. He didn't do out of school activities because he was afraid to leave her. He also realized that outside activities cost money, money he didn't see the family having.

I really couldn't argue with his reasoning. My thoughts on the matter however were that he was beginning to experience success academically, and that he should have the opportunity to experience activities with boys his own age, before attending Junior High.

The school offered a Saturday basketball league that was free of charge. School personnel donated their Saturday mornings, and the high school basketball team served as referees and scorekeepers. The boys could practice during recess so Michael would only be away from home on Saturday mornings.

Jenny was all for it. She admitted that she had tried to sign him up for other activities but he refused. It took some encouragement, it was slow in the beginning but with patience and encouragement from his classroom support network he was able to experience success.

As the school year came to a close, Michael's grades were only slightly better than his social promotion grades, but to him there was a huge difference. He had earned those grades and he had learned. Throughout the year, there were times that we talked together about his grandmother, and I also included some reminders about Faith. Jenny raised her children in the church, but Michael was just one example of a church kid who didn't realize the real power of prayer.

One summer day after school was out, I went to get the mail and there was a letter from Michael. He admitted that one of his classmates had written it for him but he dictated it. In the body of the letter he thanked me for all the extra time and effort I had put forth so that he could experience success. He admitted that it was the first time he had ever experienced success in school, or in sports. Michael thanked me for caring for him and his grandmother. He said he felt our talks about God and Faith could allow him to participate more in activities in Junior High. He concluded the letter by saying that he was sincere about this writing and that this was not just another "you are my favorite teacher" letter.

Michael was a youngster in need. God provided the answers. I was the messenger.

* * * * *

Steve was the second student of interest during that first year in town. He was an active young man with a slender athletic build. He had wavy blonde hair and sparkling blue eyes. I noticed him from time to time walking in the neighborhood after school with a elderly looking man with a cane. It wasn't until conference time after the first nine weeks that I was introduced to this gentleman. He was not as elderly as he appeared and his cane was white. He was blind as a result of advanced diabetes. He was on dialysis. He was Steve's father.

Steve like Michael experienced separation anxiety and he feared leaving his father. He had good reason to be afraid. His dad was seriously ill. He needed a kidney transplant, but in that time, they were few and very difficult to arrange. He was already past the stage of a good transplant candidate. He was just living out his remaining days.

Steve's mother was a registered nurse and was able to handle the father's medical needs. She kept Steve up to date on his father's condition. Being in the medical profession meant that she worked long hours and often Steve was alone with his dad. On occasion the ambulance would come to take his dad to the hospital. This was again way more responsibility than a twelve year old needed to deal with, but Steve was an exceptional young man.

Steve and I visited openly about his father's condition and his prognosis. He knew that his father was going to die, and we talked often about Heaven. Steven was also concerned about his mother and the toll that caring and watching a father and a husband wasting away was taking on her. I prayed for strength and acceptance for Steve and his mother.

Steven's father lived through his sixth grade year. When he entered Junior High, a home health care nurse was hired to provide assistance with his dad medical needs. This allowed the mother some relief and it gave Steve the opportunity to deal with Junior High and all of its activities. We remained close friends and talked often about his school accomplishments and his sports achievements. I continued to pray for his father and his family and for their strength to deal with the future.

Steve's father passed away during the spring semester of his seventh grade year. During the remainder of his junior high career we spent a lot of time together. Steve had an interest in journalism. At that time I was working part time for a local newspaper and was a sports broadcaster for a local radio station. I was able to arrange for Steve to participate in some of the sports programming and was able to give him some writing tips. Late in his eighth grade year his mother got married and they moved out of state.

The announcement of the move was very discouraging. Through all that had happened in his life he had his friends and his local support system to help him through. Now he was going to have to leave it all behind. I reminded him that I prayed for strength and acceptance daily and even though he had lost his father, his Heavenly Father was always available to help. He also needed a healthy dose of Faith.

The move went without incident. He actually lived closer than he thought and we were able to keep in contact through his high school years. I knew he was attending Oklahoma State University's School of Journalism, but after that I lost track of him. Years later I talked with a relative who reported that he was a college professor in the journalism department of a prestigious East Coast university.

Steven had to overcome some great adversity. God had a plan, I was the messenger.

* * * * *

The following year provided plenty of need and opportunity to minister. The next young man's notoriety preceded him. The phone at the school office was ringing all summer long. The message was direct. Please don't place my child in the same class as Stephen.

On and off during the summer I was at school and often talked with students in the up-coming class. The word on the street was that Stephen was going to be in my room in the fall. The official lists that teacher see wouldn't be released until August. It's funny, kids seemed to always know and they were always right. A number of my summer visitors felt they had also been assigned to my class and they were excited about having Stephen as a classmate.

From what I could sort out, Stephen had been a student at my school earlier in his school career but moved to a parochial school in his earlier grades to help his mom deal with his incorrigible attitude. None who could remember him were sad to see him leave. His tenure at the private school ended in failure and he was returning to our school as damaged merchandise. I'm big on second chances and I wanted to meet this young man and the sooner the better.

All Stephen's past seemed to be forgiven by the boys in the neighborhood. On my next visit to school the neighborhood boys appeared with this mystery person and casually introduced me to Stephen.

I was expecting this rough, tough, uncontrollable juvenile delinquent. To my surprise Stephen was a normal sized sixth-grader, with a very athletic build and ruffled blonde hair. He displayed a kind of a carefree disposition and seemed to be a good fit for his peers. His initial appearance was a bit rambunctious, but far from criminal. I decided at that moment to dismiss all the negatives that preceded him. If I was truly going to give him that second chance I had to be able to accept him for what he is, not for what he was.

With the opening of school, I soon realized that Stephen's actual problems were deeply rooted in family history. Steve lived in a middle class neighborhood with his mother and older brother. There was an older sister that was not living at home. Both the older siblings were problem children that were creating a handful of trouble for a mother who already suffered depression from a failed marriage. Stephen was her last hope for success and in her eyes that opportunity was fading fast.

As the school year moved along, mom's depression plunged. She was chasing her problems with prescription drugs and alcohol. One fall morning in late September a faculty member, who was a neighbor, reported that Stephen had appeared at her door in the middle of the night and reported that he had just called 911. His mother had overdosed and he was not sure she was still breathing. The ambulance arrived.

The EMT's recognized the symptoms as an overdose. They were able to stabilize her vital signs including her breathing and then took her to the hospital. Stephen didn't even want to go with her. He spent the night with the teacher / neighbor.

This was big news the next day at school. Stephen was a brave little boy who was just trying to hold his life together. He freely shared the information of the previous night. He was approaching a breaking point.

His classmates had told him that I was sincere about a second chance. I had already visited with the class about "Angels, Death, and Heaven. The students quickly referred Stephen to conference with me about his problems.

We talked about faith, hope and love. We talked about surviving and the qualities of a survivor. I prayed for him to be strong, to be tolerant, to be patient, and to practice forgiveness. Stephen was raised in the church. He was an altar boy, but he was just beginning to experience the rewards of being a Christian

His mom returned home in the next few days. I encouraged Stephen to talk with his mother. He needed to tell her his feelings about her and about how much he needed her.

Stephen told his mom that he was mad at her. Her solution to family problems utilizing drugs and alcohol was not acceptable. At the same time he emphasized how important she was to him, how much he loved her, and how much he would like to depend on her.

A month later the school held parent-teacher conferences. Stephen told me on the day of his scheduled appointment that his mother would not be attending. Much to my surprise she appeared at her appointed time. She looked rough but she made an effort to look appropriate for a meeting with her son's teacher.

When we sat down at the conference table, I silently thanked God for allowing us to meet and asked HIM for direction in our discussion.

She opened by telling the story of the overdose and the discussion she had with her son. She admitted that up to that time she was directing all of her energy to the failures in her life. She had failed to realize that the last hope she had for success was succeeding.

"When Stephen told me that he loved me and explained how much I meant to him, I decided at that moment that I was going to change," she announced.

Getting a good academic report and hearing little about poor attitudes and discipline gave her a reason to be proud. Tear filled her eyes as she prepared to leave. She offered her help if the school needed any volunteers. I'm not sure that tear's weren't in my eyes as well when she left.

The remainder of the year was not without challenges. Being a preteen boy, Stephen and his pals were going to find ways to get into mischief. I must say that he was one of the most honest students that I had in my teaching career. Stephen excelled in sports that year. He had honor roll grades and participated in my school choir.

I especially remember the Mother's Day Tea. The students performed a musical program, and served cookie and punch to their mothers and grandmothers. The program ended with the students presenting their guests with a long stem carnation.

Stephen was the proudest student in the room when he presented his mother with the flower. I could see how proud she was to be his mother. The neighborhood mothers also were quick to greet her and make her feel welcomed. Stephen had given her a reason to live.

Another happy ending!

Not exactly!

At the end of the school year Stephen and his mom moved out of the school district. He was not happy and when his grades began to fail, his mother quickly returned him to his previous school. One Saturday not long after school started I received a phone call.

Stephen's older brother got high on drug and had killed himself.

I said a quick prayer for guidance and before I knew it I was right in the middle of a family in trauma. Mother was being challenged beyond her limits.

I took Stephen for a while and made sure he had what he needed for the funeral. Suicide is a unique situation. We prayed together first for forgiveness, then for strength and acceptance. Stephen offered special prayers for his mother.

Stephen was especially missing his support group. This was the group that carried him through his mom's overdose. He greatly needed them now.

The funeral time came and went and as with most deaths life quickly returned to normal. Fortunate for Stephen, he would return to his support system when he returned to school. I kept in close touch with the family for several weeks after this traumatic event. I ask Stephen to call me if he needed to talk or needed support of any kind. I made the same offer to his mother.

Stephen played on my Boy's Club junior high basketball team, and on my AAU basketball team. He seemed to adjust quickly and I will credit that to his strong Christian background.

Stephen knew Christ. He just needed to be empowered in Christ. God provided that empowerment. I was the messenger.

* * * * *

Dusty was an 11 year old sixth grader. His broad shoulders and deep voice revealed that his physical maturity was advanced. He was short and stocky with a ruddy complexion and dusty brown hair He had an athletic look, but displayed the characteristics of a loner.

If you looked close you would notice a slight limp. His main interest was in ATV riding and he would ride for hours alone. The limp was a product of too many ATV crashes. Dusty suffered serious injury when in anger he lost control of his ATV and crashed. He was lucky to escape the accident with only a broken arm.

Socially, he was careful about choosing acquaintances. He was friendly, but had few close friends. He shared little and was somewhat mysterious. He had too much to hide.

Intellectually he performed at an average level, but showed signs of higher ability. He indicated that he saw no advantage for high academic performance. Dusty was not interested in sports, only in ATV riding.

Early in the year his mother showed an interest in Dusty's ability but she also was very quiet and somewhat evasive and didn't want to push.

Bridging The Gap

Truth to be revealed, Dusty's dad was an abusive husband and father. This would account for the mother and the son's distant position. Much of father's problems stemmed from alcoholism.

Dusty like most sons wanted a loving caring father. Early in the year he defended his father. On his own he admitted that his father had trouble holding a job. On occasions he would black out while on the job. Then he would miss work.

Dusty went through a period when he felt he could be the man of the house and would try to defend mother from father's abusive displays. Even during these periods, deep down, he felt he was selling his father out. His mother threatened to leave his father and remove Dustin from school and run. They held on until the end of the year.

I was on a class outing with Dusty to an amusement park. I was enjoying seeing him have a good time. Before the day was over he told me in the strictest confidence that tomorrow he and his mother were leaving permanently to live with relatives.

When I questioned him about his destination, he would not tell me. He admitted that it wasn't that he didn't want me to know, but he knew that if I knew and someone asked, he didn't want me to have to lie to protect him. It was like he was going into the witness protection program and I truly felt I would never see him again.

The next morning I called rather early just to say goodbye. A frantic father answered the phone and demanded that I tell him where they went. He knew I had been a source of strength for Dusty and as we talked, his attitude melted from hostile and demanding to pleading and begging. Where had they gone? He was sure that I knew.

It was at that point I knew Dusty was truly looking out for me by not telling. I understood that this was a test of faith. Tearfully the dad hung up and we both felt terrible. I knew that Dusty was gone for good and this father had, for all practical purposes lost his son. That was probably the saddest part of all.

A years later, on Thanksgiving Day my phone rang. It was Dusty. He reported that he was living in Colorado outside of Denver with relatives. He was fine, in school and enjoyed snowmobiling. His attitude seemed confident and he said his mother was working and life was improving.

They were progressing from surviving to living. Still no address and phone number but I knew he could reach me. I was still free from information.

Many years later a stocky young man with a beard appeared at school on a motorcycle. I was Dusty. He wanted to have lunch. We set is the lunchroom and visited man to man. He had graduated from high school and was still living in Colorado. He was unsure of his future but I knew he would do well. He had survived the hardest part. The rest should be easier. While I still wonder about him, and I am wondering a lot right now; I am not worried. I'm sure his faith will guide him.

This was a young man who had a strong faith, but in times of adversity he doubted. God took care of Dusty and his family. I was just the messenger.

* * * * *

Rob arrived at school in late August as a transfer student. While he had an IEP, he didn't appear to have problems and brought no negative baggage. He did have a chip on his shoulder and some days he just dared you to knock it off.

Rob really had no belief system. He lived with his mom and a step dad and a stepbrother. He seemed to just be ok with the living arrangements. He accepted the step dad and step son but was not comfortable with them.

Rob was of normal height for his age. While he possessed a compact, muscular stature, he appeared somewhat under nourished. His athletic build supported his hair trigger attitude which dared you to invade his space. He had dark hair and dark penetrating eyes reflecting a troubled existence. He had an olive complexion and facial features that indicated a possible Native American or Asian heritage.

His appearance cried out for intervention. I prayed for guidance in dealing with this one. He didn't appear to attend church or Sunday school, and it also appeared that survival was at the top of his list of priorities. Even though he seemed to have an attitude, we quickly bonded and I began working on his very weak belief system.

As I mentioned previously, Rob had an IEP (Individual Education Plan) which indicated language weaknesses and also indicated a weakness in reading. His reading and language problems were linked to dyslexia. He relied strongly on visual and auditory cues to supplement his learning.

His remedial instructor, who was very experienced and compassionate, was quick to realize these learning deficits. She also had a number of other students from my home room that needed varying degrees of assistance. Because I had several students who relied on auditory and visual cues, I had already adjusted my teaching styles to accommodate others in the class.

Rob found that making friend was not difficult and while he was still burdened with the chip on his shoulder, he seemed comfortable in his current school environment. Because I had already made changes to my teaching styles, he quickly began to fit in academically and between his special service teachers and his in class adaptations; he began to quickly experience success. He also developed an in class support system that assisted in his learning and provided additional confidence. His attendance was good. He was experiencing growth, both academically and socially.

It was conference time. I couldn't have been prouder of a student, and he was proud of himself. I encouraged him to have his mom come for the quarterly grade report. Rob reported anxiously that she would be coming. I hoped that she came, or he would be disappointed and that could set back our progress.

The appointed time came and it went and still no mother. I must admit that I was feeling anger grow within me and I knew why it was hard for Rob to trust. When I finally got a break I called the home.

I was still angry when I dialed the phone number. It rang and rang with no answer. How could she spoil the first ounce of success Rob had achieved in months, maybe years? The phone continued to ring and I was giving up on this conversation and losing hope on the whole situation.

Finally somebody picked up. A male voice answered the phone. I was not expecting a man's voice. I asked to whom I was speaking. In a very official tone the man reported that he was a member of the local police department. I asked to speak to Rob's mom. He told me that would be impossible. I told him who I was and what I wanted.

He began by telling me that the house was a crime scene and they were investigating a possible shooting. By now my mind was racing. There was no school today. Robert was at home. Following a long pause, the officer reported that the mother was in jail for attempting to shoot the stepdad. When I inquired as to injuries, the officer replied in a less serious tone that there were no injuries. He added she wasn't a very good shot. My final question was about Rob. He was safe. Family Services had taken him from home and he was in the care of a relative. That's all they would tell me.

It was a long afternoon but since it was a conference day, I finished up by mid-afternoon. It took some begging but after locating a friend at the police station I finally found where they had placed Rob.

After that day Rob was in and out of my life. In a couple of days he was returned to his mom's minus the step-dad and the step-brother. He returned to school but at the semester he transferred out.

He played on our school basketball team that played at the Boy's Club. After missing a few games he showed up at a practice. As far as his team members were concerned he had never been gone. We finished the season together and then he disappeared again.

He reappeared at the Boy's Club the next November and wanted to know if he could be on my seventh grade team. The team was almost the same team as the year previous everyone was just a year older. There was no problem with him playing and he rejoined the team.

In late February Rob missed a practice and then a game. I was a little concerned but since his situation was so unstable, there was little I could do. After he had missed two weeks of practices and games, I asked the Club director if he had any information on him.

He reported that his mother had been in a terrible automobile accident a couple of weeks ago. She was in a coma and her chances for survival were slim. The main question on my mind is, "Where is Rob?" While this whole situation was unsettling, I felt confident that he was safe and being cared for. Robert always seemed to land on his feet.

It was Palm Sunday just after church when my home phone rang. It was Rob's relatives calling from the hospital. They wanted me to meet them to discuss Rob and his mother. That was all they reported.

This situation seemed strange. I said a prayer of Thanksgiving that Robert was apparently OK, and I also said a prayer for guidance for the activities that lay before me.

When I arrived at the hospital I was met by a large group of family members. They began by assuring me that Rob was fine and would be along later in the day. If he wasn't here, then why did I need to be here?

An additional family member appeared and announced that the doctor was now ready to speak to the family. They insisted that I hear what he had to say.

His report was very grim. Rob's mom had been in the hospital for over a month in a coma. She was suffering from a severe head injury. Her condition had not changed. Her brain function appeared minimal. The doctors had called the family together to make a decision. They felt that it was time to take her off life support. This would most likely result in her death. It might be hours, but certainly death would come within days.

The family turned to me. They had made the decision to turn off the machines that were prolonging a life. The wanted me to tell Robert that his mother was going to die.

Before I could speak they pointed out that he would have little to do with any of the family and he talked about me as someone he trusted and respected. They knew he would be devastated, but he had to know. They had asked that she be left connected until after her son's evening visit.

This was my biggest assignment yet. I told the family that I was going to the chapel and would meet them in the waiting room to wait for Rob. God's instructions were to do as I was asked. I was to relate the doctor's opinions and also his prediction that she would die. This young man was so young and had been through so much and now this. Here I was again smack in the middle of a traumatic, life changing experience. I really didn't know what to do or say.

When Rob arrived, he walked into the room with his sure, confident gait. A family spokesman point out my presence and he appeared pleased to see me. I was afraid that seeing me would make him anxious, but why should it. My presence in the past had always been a good thing. That was about to change.

Other family members cleared out leaving Rob and me alone. I spoke quietly. I related what the doctor had told us about his mother and I concluded with the doctors expectations. By now my voice was cracking and tears blurred my eyes. He listened very attentively. I finished by telling him he probably should say his goodbyes. The doctor said once she was taken off life support, the end should come quickly.

I let him go in on his own. When he returned he was agitated.

He yelled, "I'm not telling her good-by, she ain't gonna die! God won't let her die!"

That was the first time I'd ever heard him reference God. That was the best thing that happened all day.

When he left his mother's room he turned on me. He yelled at me as tears streamed down his face.

"You're the biggest hypocrite I've ever met," He screamed!" You're not a believer, you're a quitter!"

By now he was crying uncontrollably and collapsed in my arms. I evidently wasn't to comforting. In a short time he broke away, and pushed me away.

His last words to me, "I don't ever want to see you again."

I wasn't surprised. I knew when I accepted the challenge from the family that it could end like this. It was a gamble, but at least maybe I flushed out some of his anger and disappointment. It was easier for me to take the heat and not his relatives. Those were the people that would have to help him rebuild his life.

Robert took off on a run. I just let him go. He knew his way around the hospital and probably just needed some alone time. I reported back to his aunts and uncles. I told them what he had said, but I also let them know that I had delivered the doctors grim message.

By now it was well into the night. I was exhausted. I made my way to the chapel before leaving for home. That part of the hospital was quiet. When I reached the entrance to the chapel and looked inside I was startled to see Robert up front. He was quietly praying. I couldn't hear what he was saying, but for today, my prayers were answered.

Robert had found God. I didn't know how things were going to turn out with his mother but I knew he was now in good hands and I had been the messenger.

This story does have a happy ending. The mom lasted until Easter Sunday. On that day she was visited by a faith healer who "laid on hands."

Later that evening she came out of the comma. A couple of weeks in rehab and she was on her way home.

I happened to run into one of Rob's aunts while out shopping. She told me of her sister's miraculous recovery. What wonderful news! They thanked me for my efforts with Rob. I was apparently still in the dog house with him, but they felt it would pass. To this day I haven't seen Rob or his mother.

* * * * *

Anna was a bright sixth grade girl. She was popular, but hadn't broken into the "in" group of girls. She was a very independent young lady and she didn't feel the need to be in that group.

Her particular talent was in music and she had a beautiful voice. She sang at church and in both the honor chorus and the chorus I provided for our sixth grade students.

She lived at home with her family, the father who was a businessman, an entrepreneur of sorts, and her mother who worked in the medical field. She had two brothers, one older and one younger. She was being raised in a good Christian home.

Come conference day both mom and dad attended. This was different because on many occasions the dad was out of town on business. I would often see him at game with the boys and we were friends, I was just not used to seeing him at school. The parents seemed stressed which was also different. Their children had always been good students and there was no reason to expect anything different this time

When we all sit down at the conference table the parents wasted no getting right to the point.

The mother cleared her throat and spoke, "In the next few weeks there are going to be changes in our family. I'm afraid that these changes will affect the children."

The first thing I thought of was divorce. How could this family be going through that? They all worked together so well. They never seemed to be issues from home that spilled over into school. It was such a well-adjusted family. It surely must be something else.

The mother continued. "In the next few weeks, the children's father will be going away for a while. His absence will actually be for a number of years."

I must have had a confused look on my face, but the mother continued. Tears stained her face as she explained how her husband had promoted some business and had some-how got cross-ways with the government. In the coming weeks he would be going on trial, and the outcome would most likely result in him being sentenced to several years in a federal penitentiary.

The results of this situation would require the family to move to more modest living quarters and the children would probably have to accept benefits afforded low income families.

This would definitely require home adjustments. The parents were waiting to tell the children until they were sure that the prison sentence was to become reality. They just wanted me to be alert to the situation. They felt that Anna might be more in need of attention because of her independent ways and the fact that she was more sensitive than the boys.

In about a month, the sentence was handed down and lives did change. It was the talk or gossip that was the worst. There were judgments that were forced on the family and the children. Fortunately, the family's church members stood solidly behind them.

These adjustments were hard on all of the children. The boys were hurting also. I offered prayers daily and proceeded as God guided me. It broke my heart when the children were excited about spending spring break in a city near the prison so they could spend time with their father.

During the remainder of her sixth grade year Anna immersed herself in the music that she dearly loved. She enjoyed singing for her church and I was delighted that she would lend us her voice for the Free Spirit Singers, the choir I directed.

When she entered Junior High, her withdrawal continued. By the time she got to high school she had become almost a complete introvert. She allowed herself to participate in the musical activities at the school but by the time she was a junior she had endured all the judgmental comments and remarks she could take.

She quit school and got her G.E.D. She then took the ACT and received a high enough score to receive a scholarship to any public university in Missouri. She attended college but her true interest was in singing. She eventually found her way to Nashville where she was able to get a taste of what the music industry was like. She returned to college and received degrees in music and is now a singer and songwriter.

I had the privilege of attending wedding ceremonies for Anna at her home. It was good to see her and the family back together again. It was also heartwarming to see this family stand in support of the father's adverse situation and welcome him back home.

Many times since I had Anna in school I would talk to her mother and we would talk about her grade school days. I am honored when her mother includes me in Anna's successes. I also appreciated the family's thanks for helping them adjust in their time of need.

These children had some great hurdles to overcome. Their faith may have wavered a bit, but they were survivors in Christ. I was just the messenger.

* * * * *

Matt and I became acquainted at the beginning of sixth grade. He was a good student and he was all-boy. He was very bright, very popular, and very athletic. Matt also had a very strong Christian background. I enjoyed having him in class and would attend some of his athletic competitions. I would see his family on game nights and on family activity nights at school. His mother was a high school teacher.

His solid Christian background received a huge challenge when his young father died from a heart attack following an early morning swim at their home pool. Knowing the family and their relationship with the Lord, I knew that this would be tough, but I was sure they could handle it. I had discussed death and dying with my class as usual. Matt was in junior high now but I knew that even for a kid he was strong in his Christian beliefs.

Since Matt was now in Junior High and since this was such a huge shock to the family I did not go to the house prior to the funeral. He had a strong group of junior high students for peer support and the support of his church.

When I arrived at the funeral home, the chapel was full. Being on a weekday, many students were not in attendance, but many of the teachers were there to support Matt's mother.

The service began with some uplifting scripture and a kind supportive eulogy. During the sermon part of the service, the spiritual leader described the father's future as "being placed in the cold, hard ground. He would exist in the lifeless, dark tomb until the end of the world when God called all believers home."

That explanation of death sent chills up my spine. That's nothing like I experienced. Matt responded to this declaration from the clergy in charge with a flash of anger followed by sobbing.

I so wanted to get to him. I wanted to comfort him with the good news that his father was no longer a part of what was going into the ground. From where I was sitting it was difficult to get to the front. By the time I was anywhere close, the funeral directors had whisked the casket away and the body was on its way to the cemetery.

As disappointed as I was about how the service ended, I paused for a moment to think about what had happened. As startling as a destination of cold, hard ground for the rest of earthly time was, it's possible that it was part of the doctrine of that religion. Maybe that's what their version of Christianity expected. Still it seemed such a harsh realization for a youngster.

Since the service took place during school time I had to pass on the cemetery service and I returned to school. This harsh, dismal position on death left me deeply troubled for the remainder of the day. All I could remember was seeing Matt break down in tears. I just couldn't let it go.

As I traveled home I asked that God give me some comfort and that he would guide my actions as to how to handle Matt's situation. I went home and was going to have dinner. I would then visit Matt and his family at their home. As I sat at the dinner table picking at my food I kept waiting for this declaration from above as to what I should do next. What was I going to say?

All too soon I was pulling into the driveway at Matt's house. There were several visitors, mostly relatives. Matt's mom answered the door and thanked me for coming. As I followed her to Matt's room she told me how hard he was taking this ordeal. She said that he had asked about me and assured me that he would welcome my visit.

She knocked on his door and announced my presence. As Matt answered the door, he again broke into tears. As the closed behind us I knew I was in the right place.

We shared comforting words and a more acceptable view of death. I told Matt that my experience with death was painless and immediate. The spirit passed from the body at the time of death, and continued to exist in a state of total mobility; an all inclusive state that keeps you closely linked to your earthly family and loved ones. Matt sobbing tapered off and I could see relief on his face.

I stayed and we visited and shared for almost an hour. I reminded him that with God's help he will overcome this trauma in his life. I also reassured him that God and his father would both be close by for all of his earthly existence.

Matt felt troubled and angry about the loss of his father. God gave him strength. I was the messenger.

* * * * *

For twenty year of my thirty year public school tenure I work in a self-contained setting where I had the same group of students all day. The last ten years I worked in a departmental setting where I taught a different group of students each period. It seemed to me that having less contact with particular students made in more difficult to relate to them.

Following are two examples of interventions from my later years.

* * * * *

Travis was a very good-natured young man; his main interest was youth wrestling. He had been competing in tournaments since he was in first grade and he was very good. He was small but compact. Travis was very muscular, and very strong. He was a good student who demonstrated positive work principles.

He had supportive parents and supportive family members. He reflected good positive family values. He attended church regularly and openly exhibited good Christian ethics.

After Christmas vacation I began to notice a difference in Travis's demeanor. He seemed moody, tense, and on edge. He also began losing weight and his appearance turned pale. His grade started to slip, and his attitude became complacent, with flares of anger. He was missing school.

These changes were alarming. His eyes which usually were sparkling and reflected his ornery side had lost their luster. They seemed dull and lifeless and begged for help. I caught up with him after lunch one day and we talked.

When questioned about the changes he told me that he was tired all the time; he had no energy. He was seeing a doctor; that explains his absences. So far they could find no causes for his health issues.

These symptoms sounded serious. I felt compelled to call Travis's mother. She agreed to meet with me later that day when she picked him up after school.

She began by expressing thanks to me for being so observant and for being such a good listener. She said that Travis had wanted to talk to somebody about his health issues, but he didn't want the whole school to know. She confessed that Travis might have leukemia. He had been having weekly blood tests but his counts remained abnormal.

He had an appointment at the hospital for extensive testing that would either rule out the presence of cancer or that would confirm its presence. The tests were scheduled over Spring Break. That was still two weeks away. Mom said that the waiting was impossible, but the worst part of the deal was that he couldn't wrestle until after he was released by the doctor.

For the next two weeks we visited at lunch and before and after class. Most of his peers were not aware of his condition but most knew something was not right. Travis would not voluntarily pass on wrestling practice and he had already missed three matches. During our talks we visited about all of the possibilities. We were praying for no cancer and answers for the existing symptoms.

I was reminded of times after the accident when I was facing unpleasant realities, I always looked at both side of the problem so I would be prepared to face life, and whatever the reality might be. I tried to talk straight-up to Travis. I wanted him to know that a cancer diagnosis was not a death sentence. He would need strength and courage to preserve his quality of life if he received a negative report.

We visited one last time before the spring break. We prayed together for strength and courage. I was scheduled to be in Florida, with a school group, during his testing but I assured him that I would be praying for him. I insisted that he keep praying and that he be brave.

I kept my promise and prayed for Travis daily. The morning of his tests, I prayed a special prayer. He was on my mind for the entire day. When I returned to the hotel that evening, I rested while the chaperones took the students swimming.

My rest was interrupted by the ring of my cell phone. I answered and on the other end of the conversation was Travis's mom. She was relieved to report that his test all came back alright. His blood count was mysteriously returning towards normal. His prognosis was that he would gradually regain his strength and his weight. Most important of all, he would wrestle again.

We shared some tears of joy together and I thanked her for calling. She said Travis insisted that she call as soon as they knew the results but she told him that I would be busy until later in the evening. She said that he also wanted me to know that he was brave.

God gave Travis Faith and Courage. I was the messenger.

* * * * *

Daniel was a different kind of student. He was very quiet and it seemed like in the classroom he didn't want to be noticed. He suffered a disability that made learning difficult. Even with his learning problems he still maintained a positive cheerful attitude. He was well liked by his peers. His peers were his support group that helped him keep up academically.

He was a small-framed lightweight. He was also a wrestler. He was tall and lanky, but very solid. Wrestling was his claim to fame and while he was not always a champion, he never gave up and was a good prospect as a high school grappler.

His parents were good church going people who worked hard to provide for their family. They were understanding of Daniels needs and very supportive of his wrestling activities.

On a February afternoon while participating in a class discussion, Daniel, raised his hand. When I called on him he was gasping and struggling to get a breath. He was stout, but fortunately he was not heavy and I was able to get him into the hallway. A fellow teacher who was on the safety committee began administering the Heimlich maneuver. When she was unsuccessful she asked me to try.

As I grasped the young man, I knew he was in trouble. As he struggled to force air into his lungs, his muscular system and his nervous system were starting to fail. He was struggling to stay standing. His skin was clammy and cold. He was fighting to stay alive. His lips were blue.

One more upward thrust under his rib cage and he frantically gapped one last time. This time he swallowed. His choking action was immediately replaced with coughing and eventually his breathing began to even out. His skin color returned and he was completely aware of the present.

As his coughing let up, he calmly brushed himself off and asked if he could get a drink. He washed his face and we returned to class. Life goes on.

Neither of us especially wanted to discuss the situation, we just wanted to get back to normal. As the day drew to an end the story was all over the school. Daniel was painting me as some kind of Hero.

I certainly didn't feel; like a Hero. But for just one desperate second I held the difference between life and death in my hands. The feeling of life slipping away is indescribable. The sensation of life returning is unforgettable. I am thankful for Daniel's life, and I'm thankful for the experience of Life and Death.

In this lifetime drama, Daniel needed saving. God was the director; I was just one of the actors.

* * * * *

These individual accounts represent only a small fraction of the service opportunities God afforded me during my teaching career. Like situations are placed before all of us on a regular basis. I approach them with a total trust that God's guidance will provide acceptable results.

Pray for incite to recognize situations. Pray for acceptance to understand situations. Pray for strength, wisdom and courage to resolve situations.

CHAPTER 15

BREAKING POINT

"In the spring of 1971, God scraped my soul off of the asphalt near Branson, Missouri. His message was clear: You will work with young people and you will make a difference in their lives. For the past thirty years I have lived up to that directive..."

-words from my retirement speech in May of 2002-

For the last 30 years I had made good on my efforts to make a difference in the lives of young people, but in one year, my world seemed to come crashing down on me.

Several things contributed to my collapse in confidence.

The last few years of my tenure I had become involved in the politics of the school. The superintendent at that time professed to be of strong Christian character, but as his service time unfolded he was driven by one thing: his own personal success. He was consumed with power. He was running over anyone and anything that failed to subscribe to his narrow view of right.

That included students, parents and employees.

The school that I had dedicated the last 30 years of my life to was no more than a "brain mill" with a single goal: pass the state test. The "Boss" used the federal "no child left behind" mandate to validate his fanatical actions. What people seemed to forget was, when you put all of these children in line, there may be no child left behind, but there will always be those at the front of the line and those at the end of the line.

My position as president of the local teachers' association placed me in the unfortunate position of protecting teachers' rights. While I could talk a good talk, the truth of the matter was that the "Boss" did whatever he wanted. He hired who he wanted and he fired who he wanted. The personal rights and the opportunity for true personal growth in the school district were being trampled. The idea that teachers had rights and they could be protected was a myth.

Time after time the teacher's association failed in their attempt to mediate situations involving teachers' rights or self-serving district policies. Most attempts at resolution also were followed by attempts to retaliate.

My involvement in teachers' association activities was a growing source of anxiety, disappointment, and in some cases anger. Problems, stemming from school politics, were affecting my ability to work with youngsters. It was also interfering in my personal and family growth and dynamics.

> "God grant me the serenity to accept the things I cannot change; courage to change the things I can; and wisdom to know the difference."

I was losing the wisdom to tell the difference. But that was not the driving reason for my retirement.

* * * * *

That story began a few days before the start of school in 2001. A frantic mother arrived for a conference concerning her son. She wanted me to understand that her son, Jake, would be in my classroom the coming year and there were some things I needed to know about him. Then for the next 15 minutes she proceeded to paint a picture of her son as a teenage juvenile delinquent who had temper flares and was often out of control. She said his physical strength and his periods of violent behavior could make him dangerous.

When she finished I did my best to reassure her that I would look out for his welfare and expressed my thanks that she chose to share this information with me. She reminded me as she left that sometimes she was afraid to be alone with him.

There were three other teachers in my team. I scheduled a meeting to discuss Jake with them. Our team members all shared a concern for students and while they listened to the mother's assessment of her son, we were skeptical as to his true personality. When I asked the principal and the school counselor about particulars on this child, they admitted that this was the first they had heard of him. Jake's history was discouraging but I had a roster of other students that also needed attention.

The bell rang on the first day of school. I closed the door and looked out over this year's group of homeroom students. It looked like a promising group. I scanned the faces of these youngsters looking for Jake. I was sure he would stand out. I expected a large well developed, red faced young man who was overly active and in someone's face. I saw no one fitting that description. Maybe he transferred to another class; maybe to another school.

I searched my roster and there was his name. I called the roll. To my surprise he was a tall slender young man who was squeezed into his desk at the corner of the room far from me. He displayed none of the characteristics the mother had outlined. He looked tired and anxious. He was quiet and withdrawn. His speech was soft and cautious. My first thought was he was medicated.

At the end of the day our teaching team met specifically to discuss Jake. We were all of the opinion that his initial behavior was due to medication. When I checked with the nurse the mom had reported no regular meds.

* * * * *

In the midst of this personal intervention, perhaps the greatest single challenge to democracy was playing out on the East Coast of our nation. Terrorists had hi-jacked four commercial jets, destroyed the Word Trade Center in New York, caused significant damage to the Pentagon in Washington D.C., and the final plane was crash landed in a field in Pennsylvania, preventing an attack on the White House.

I stood before my class that day with tears running down my cheeks. I explained, "the tears you see on my face are not tear of fear, and not tears of sadness, but tears of pride for a nation with a history of survival and tears of Faith in a God that takes care of his Own."

We were a nation of Survivors.

* * * * *

As the weeks passed Jake's demeanor changed very little. He had poor study habits, poor organization skills, and in general a poor outlook on life. He expressed frustration but never approached anger. After the fifth week, his progress remained poor and we contacted the mother for a conference. We outlined some activities that could help improve his organizational skills and his study habits. We suggested another conference at the end of the grading period.

Her side of the conference was a continuation of an attack on his character. She told us that he showed no responsibilities at home. He would not do his homework. All he wanted to do was talk back and be disagreeable. She didn't know how we tolerated his behavior.

Our conference time had expired. When she left I began to equate a lot of his characteristics as those of a normal middle school boy with just a touch of drama. My co-workers and I decided that we would address his responsibility problems and discuss some homework ideas. I even went as far as giving him helpful hints on how to get along with his mom.

In the next few weeks I began to work closely with Jake. We discussed what it was like to be a survivor. We discussed terms like faith and hope. During this time he became more settled. I helped him work out a chart for time at home that included time for chores and homework. We talked daily. I encouraged him to discuss things that were troubling in his life.

He confided that he and his mom did argue a lot. He never indicated that he fought or became violent during these arguments.

I can't speak about changes that could have occurred at home, but his school progress was outstanding. He was not honor roll material yet, but he was earning, solid average grades. He had also convinced me that he was helping out at home and he was obviously doing his homework. This was the type of turn around you couldn't wait to discuss at conferences.

The mom set down at the conference table, looked at the grades and seemed somewhat surprised and for a moment indicated just a slight bit of pride. Then she folded the grade card put it in the envelope and proceeded to outline a new list of things that were not satisfying to her. When questioned about the chores and the homework, she agreed that he was doing better, but they were still constantly at each other's throat.

This was not at all what I had expected. Jake had made the comment once that it didn't matter how hard he tried, his mother would never be happy with him. I was beginning to believe it. After that conference he did report that his mom was happy with his grades. That was the first time since school started that he seemed to be happy.

For the remainder of the semester Jake would continue to experience periods of happiness. On the other hand, sometimes he would go through periods of extreme depression. He would only say that he and his mother were not getting along. Academically he was improving. That was enough to make me smile. At the end of the semester Jake seemed to be working out his issues and his grades were improving so the team did not see a reason for a conference.

I enjoyed my Christmas Break. Part of that enjoyment was knowing that Jake had overcome his problems. With the other things going on in school, I needed something to smile about. He had built a solid academic platform the first semester and was ready to build on it in the spring. Things were working out at home and his future was looking bright.

Returning to school, I was anxious to see how my students had weathered the Break. I was especially anxious to hear about Jake's Christmas. I was disappointed when he wasn't there that first day. He was also absent the second day. He must be sick, or maybe they went on a trip and were late returning.

After lunch my question was answered. The counselor came by my room with a transfer slip for Jake. I immediately became anxious and worrisome about his future, but rationalized that he was so much more prepared than he was when school started. I envisioned him as a survivor.

The story that followed was anything but encouraging. The transfer was to an orphanage. His mom had surrendered her parental right over Christmas Break. Her live-in boyfriend gave her an ultimatum:" get rid of Jake, or I'm out of here."

I was completely devastated. I couldn't even talk. I'm sure there were tears, and God took a beating.

"How could you let something like this happen? Jake was a good boy and had shown great resilience over the last several months. He had learned to cope with aversion and to deal with it. He didn't deserve to be abandoned, and at Christmas." I rambled.

I took time for me to regain my composure and return to class. I was hurt. I had invested a lot in this boy. I couldn't even explain to the rest of the class why Jake had left. When I would try my voice would crack and I would start to tear up. The students had to accept that he just moved on.

As the year reached an end I made a decision that I could no longer fight the politics of teaching and the tyranny of the educational system. School related issues had completely destroyed our family. Finally, I could no longer work in a school setting where you lead students in the right direction, you build faith and instill hope and then watch as their DREAM is destroyed.

> *"God grant me the serenity to accept the things I cannot change; courage to change the things I can; and wisdom to know the difference."*

Those were the closing words from my retirement speech I made before my friends, my students, and my co-workers. My wife and I both were a part of that closure activity. It was not the way I envisioned the end of our thirty year career in education.

CHAPTER 16

DOWN BUT NOT OUT

I made a conscious irreversible decision to retire with my wife at the end of the school year, in late February, following the incident with Jake. I had a student teacher that last semester. In the months to follow I was able to spend time tying up loose ends to a thirty year career in teaching. I was also able devote some family time to help our oldest daughter Rebecca plan her wedding. These activities provided relief from the school related issues that seemed to keep me down.

I liked the idea of new beginnings. Rebecca was to begin her new life together with Brett after their wedding in May. She wanted her wedding be held at the lake at the Girl Scout camp where she had spent so many summers with her meemo, her mother and her sister. We worked diligently on that project and by May 11th we had everything under control but the weather. The clouds parted about two hours before the ceremony, and we enjoyed a bright and sunny afternoon for their special occasion.

Following the retirement reception, the school year ended as they always do except this year I cleaned out my desk collected my stuff and said good-bye to colleagues I had worked with for years. I admit it was a sad time. It was sad that I would miss working with these people; it was not sad that I would no longer be working in the public schools. There were no parties, no celebrations, and no special recognition of this monumental event, just the end.

Retirement challenges came early. School had been out for only a few days. Vicki and I were doing yard work when the phone rang. It was Rebecca. She was very emotional and it was hard to understand her. She reported that Rick, Brett's dad had been killed in an industrial accident. He worked for an asphalt paving company. Apparently he slipped while working and fell in front of an automated paving machine. The machine crushed him to death.

Death is so difficult to accept at any age. What a challenge for these young people! Brett idolized his dad and giving him up just as he assumed the role of a family man made it even more difficult for him to understand. Arrangements were difficult because Brett's step mom was the one responsible for making the funeral plans. Brett was pretty much left out. Because of the dysfunctional state of his family, this was a very painful and difficult event. Brett was left on the outside looking in.

Again, God was called on to silently intervene.

Vicki and I reached out to Brett as best we could. The dynamics of the multiple families seemed to only intensify the grief. This was an early challenge for their young marriage. We had acquired a son. He was suffering and hurting. Vicki and I could provide only limited relief. My daughter with God's help did the most to carry him through this tragedy.

Another new beginning came to pass in early June when Sarah our youngest announced that she had accepted a teaching position in a neighboring school district. I remember that in her retirement card to us she wrote that as we were completing our careers in education, she was just beginning hers.

Travel was on our agenda that first year after retirement. An early September trip took us to Washington D.C. and the Grand Opening of the National Museum of the American Indian. Being charter members of the museum we had experienced its development from the planning stage and were anxious for this special opening. I was honored to represent my tribe by marching in the parade of nations. It was special to attend the Grand Opening Reception with tribal representatives from around the nation.

In January we travelled to Las Vegas to celebrate the wedding anniversary of Scott and Adele. They were very special friends who lived in Florida and worked for Disney World. They'd ask us to stand up for them when they were married in Vegas, but our teaching obligations prevented that from happening. We looked forward to helping them celebrate this year. As it turned out Scott's children also joined us. We hadn't seen Lance and Lesle since they moved to Florida. It was a wonderful time for renewing friendships.

To try and beat the February blues Vicki and I flew to South Texas. We spent a week with my Aunt Betty and my cousin Daniel. They were regular winter Texans. We had visited them more than once when we would travel to meet my parents on South Padre Island. This was a very special place for my mother, and I always felt closer to her when I was on the Island.

Traveling was nice and it was good to get away. But the travel opportunities were just a diversion. When I returned home, the world after retirement remained the same. I still held bitter resentment toward school officials, society and the state of education in general. I felt that I had failed. I had led Jake in the wrong direction and it cost him his family. My retirement was developing into a pity party over my seeming inability to make that difference that I felt so confident in doing for the past thirty years.

The birth of Richard Calvin did more than anything that first year of retirement to give my life meaning. God created grandchildren to help adults solve their problems and to give life meaning. In the months following retirement I needed help. The birth of Little Calvin also did much to help heal the hurt for Brett. Children are the best medicine when it comes to healing.

As Vicki and I settled in after are travels we noticed more sunshine and warm breezes, reminders that spring was not far away. Returning from the island environment it was time to begin the preparation for Easter and the observance of lent. It was during this time of personal reflection that I realized the burdens I had carried with me those months since my school departure.

A closer evaluation showed that like everything else in my life, God had provided signs, a kind of for-shadowing in both the school issues and in particular the situation involving Jake. In both cases I was drifting from direction and trying to be the boss.

The culture and society dictated a different kind of teaching. This new educational agenda failed to recognize personal growth and achievement. The only measures of success were quantitative. That type of measure was equally successful in reporting failures. The signs were there for me as a teacher as well as a personal mentor. Those were just things I had no control over.

In Jake's case, maybe I didn't lead him the wrong way. The dissolution of his family was out of my control. The work on his belief system and developing an ability to be resilient was just preparation for a new chapter in his life. It was not one he asked for, but considering the family he had, there was surely something better in the future. I at least had some satisfaction in knowing that he knew of hope and faith, and he displayed the qualities of a "Survivor."

As God continues to remind us, there is a time and a place for everything. Sometimes our timing is just off. I knew when I retired God was going to have to take control of by reeling life. It took almost a year for me to get it back together. In that interim he slowly guided the lives of me and my loved ones. I knew if I asked he would understand. I just had to listen carefully and search hard.

It took a year of wandering to get me back to even. Does this sound familiar? Has my life been at this "Crossroads" before? What Now?

CHAPTER 17

WINDS OF CHANGE

This Sunday began no different than most that Spring. I noticed when I went out for the newspaper; it was pleasantly warm even for the early morning. It was muggy and breezy with variable clouds. Browsing the morning paper I noticed warnings of potentially damaging thunderstorms and even tornados. How many other times had we weathered those same spring day warnings?

Vicki and I drove separate cars to church that morning. We usually ride together but today our differing schedules required that we drive separately. When we left for church that day, we had no idea that we would never return to live in our house again.

On the church calendar Easter Day had past but we were still in the Easter season. This particular Sunday the theme was change. How many of you would like to embark on a new journey with your savior? How many of you would like to put the past behind and begin all anew. How many of you know what God's plan is for you?

That Sunday I was especially vulnerable. This challenge of God's plan was confusing. I was more confused than I had been since my "heavenly experience" thirty plus years ago. I was losing my way. I knelt in prayer that Sunday and ask that God would give me that direction, that he would give me that new start.

After church I took the girls and little Calvin to lunch as was tradition. Vicki was at work at SAM's Club. Little Calvin usually came home with me after church to spend the night with Nanna and Pappy. Since I had a mission trip meeting later in the afternoon he had to go home with his mother. After lunch I had some errands to run and the girls went their separate ways. Little Calvin had to go home. That was sad.

I attended the mission trip meeting I was attending with Ida Faye and Richard. They were two of our closest friends. We had been through a lot with the Ogles. This mission trip was sponsored by a local Baptist church, one of the area's largest congregations.

Since my experience at church earlier in the day, I seemed more interested in broadening my mind. I had this new found desire to search for how similar religions are and how we all serve the same God. The meeting was very informative and we were getting close to the departure date. Little did I know about all that would take place in the next three weeks?

The meeting ended about 5:00 p.m. Vicki would be getting off work soon. The Ogles suggested that we meet for dinner. We decided to meet at SAM's Club. When I left the meeting I noticed that the cloud cover had increased and the air was extremely hot and humid. The winds had dramatically increased. The dark clouds in the western sky were beginning to hide the sun.

When we arrived at SAM's the tornado sirens were blaring and we hurried to get inside. People were being cautioned to stay inside. While there was a wall of TV's in the store, none were able to receive local weather. The sirens continued to wail and information began to filter in via cell phones. While we were in no immediate danger at the store, there were confirmed tornados in the area.

By the time Vicki got off work the sirens had stopped. Since we had three cars we decided to eat on at a local hamburger joint on the north side of Joplin. It would be on the way home for us and for the Ogles. When we left the store the skies were mostly cloudy, but the clouds were breaking up in the west. They still looked rough. The air was cooler and the winds were calm.

Calvin Cassady

As we headed towards our dinner destination we noticed a lot of emergency vehicle traffic. Ambulances and fire truck were all passing us as we traveled north. When we reached the restaurant, it had no electricity. We also were hearing on the radio that the community where we lived had sustained major damage from a tornado.

We parked one vehicle at restaurant and began working our way home. Richard went with me in my Explorer; Ida and Vicki followed in our van. Once I left the lot at the restaurant I was locked in traffic. The roadway was four lanes and both north bound lanes were bumper to bumper. Emergency vehicles continued to pick their way through the congestion. When we finally made it to our connecting highway and turned east toward towards home, the traffic was worse. The eastbound roadway was only two lanes and it was jammed in both directions. We were forced to drive on the paved shoulder to allow emergency traffic the right of way. It took almost 45 minutes to travel the five miles to reach the road into our town.

When we arrived, the road was blocked and we had to show proof of residence to get past. Those manning the roadblock urged us to proceed with caution as there were numerous downed trees and power lines. They could not guarantee that we could reach our house. They suggested that we might have to park our car and walk.

As we rounded the big curve into town, the scenery was heart breaking. Huge tree were everywhere, many blocking the roadways. Some were on houses and buildings. Some were on cars. There were downed electric lines everywhere. Some were sparking and smoking. Traffic was close to a stand-still.

I was beginning to have an anxious, sinking feeling. We continued slowly and cautiously. Eventually I had to switch to four-wheel drive and leave the roadway to avoid trees and power lines. With every minute that went by I became more anxious. By the time Richard and I reached my address I had accepted the fact that this time the storm had hit home. Vicki and I were victims.

When I opened the car door I was so thankful that I had not come home alone. To see that kind destruction for the first time was not something one should experience by one's self. I was also thankful that

Ida was with Vicki. I was worried about them as they left the restaurant soon after us and they were nowhere in sight.

I was worried about my girls, Rebecca and Sarah. The cell phone circuits were already faltering and I couldn't reach anyone. I was overcome with emotion as I entered the demolished structure I immediately broke down in tears. Richard was there for comfort and to keep me in real time.

It was just a few moments. I doubted. I was worried. Then I reaffirmed the fact that God was bigger than any of this. I surrendered this problem to His care.

The house had sustained major structural damage. It moved from its foundations and the walls were leaning, some in and some out. The windows were blown out. The roof was lifted from the rafters and in many cases it was completely missing, leaving large opening to the outside.

Where were my cats? None were visible. It was starting to get dark? Where was my wife? She didn't need to see this, not tonight.

All of these thoughts were racing through my mind. I kept trying to call but no answer. The circuits were all over loaded. Be patient. You'll have to wait.

Evening was slipping into night. You could see the moon and the stars through the openings in the roof. Calm had replaced the turmoil of the ravaging storm. My family had been spared.

Finally my phone ring broke the night quiet. My wife had been locked out. They would not let her through the road blocks. She tried several different entries into town. Finally she was allowed through. She had been calling but couldn't get connected.

When she took a breath, I said everything I could think of to discourage her from coming to the house.

She was coming and nothing was stopping her. When she arrived she had already seen a lot of destruction and her long wait and some of the radio accounts had prepared her for what she was about to see.

When she arrived it was dark. We searched through the debris but could find only one working flashlight. I felt much better when she arrived. Vicki was emotionally moved by what she saw but she was the strong one. I wanted to tell her that things would be alright, but instead I had an emotional overload and again broke down. She was there as always to calm me and pick me up.

Ida and Richard urged us to come home with them. We could get some sleep and come back in the morning to decide what to do next.

I was dark with no electricity and the night time brought with it a chill. We were both in shock. Reluctantly we left our home, the place we raised our children, thirty years of memories. We left one car at the house and took the Ogles to get their car.

On the way to Ogles I called our insurance agent to initiate our claim. It was midnight and I was sure I would reach voice mail. I selected my words carefully to report the claim clearly and accurately. When a person answered the phone we pulled off the road to make sure the call would be completed.

A kind, catastrophe claim agent, listened carefully and calmly assured me that they would take care of my family. She suggested that we find a hotel for the short term and get what we needed to survive the immediate future. She promised an agent would visit us in the morning.

For the first time since we left SAM's we realized that we were famished. We stopped at The Pancake Hut, the only place left opened. Dinner turned out to be breakfast and when we finally got to the Ogles' it was close to 2:00 a.m.

As I lay in bed reflecting on the day's activities, evidence of God's planning was everywhere. We both drove to church. That removed both cars from sure destruction. I should have been home when the storm hit, instead I was at the mission trip meeting. My grandson would have been at home with me, instead his mom needed to take him home. I thanked God for caring for us all. The thought of going to bed homeless was enveloped in God's love and his promises for the future.

CHAPTER 18

THE DAY AFTER

The night was short but the sleep was great. I awoke suddenly in a strange place and the peace of the night was abruptly replaced with the crashing reality. It was like the day after the death of a loved one. You are faced with a tremendous loss and overwhelming challenges with no plan of action. These are times when we who are Christians are comforted by the certainty of God's presence.

We arrived at the house. It was 8:00 a.m. As Vicki and I walked around our property, assessing the damage from the street, we met a familiar face. It was the pastor who would be leading the mission trip. He came to tell us that the church was available for any kind of assistance. He also consoled us and assured us that the people at his church would be praying for us.

The sun was shining and the sound of chain saws filled the air. Trucks and trailers for recovering keepsakes were in yards and blocked the streets making passage difficult. Utility trucks had the right of way as they had to deal with leaking natural gas, lost telephone service and a massive power outage.

When Vicki and I arrived, much of our front yard had already been cleared. My cousin, Sharon and her husband Bill and people who I didn't even know were hard at work making firewood out of the downed trees that block our front entrance and that were scattered randomly around our front yard.

As we made our way inside, Leroy and Joan, Vicki's dad and stepmom were busy trying to salvage items from the damaged shell that had been our home. Ida and Richard joined our crew. Ida worked on the inside; Richard helped with the outside work. Eric, one of Ida's sons also joined the outside workers.

The entire town was without electricity. It was going to be days, even weeks before power would be restored to the whole town. Bill loaned us a generator to keep the refrigerator and the freezer powered up. We kept our telephones charged by using a car charger. We could only work during daylight hours. We were also at the mercy of the weather. While the day started sunny, rain and possibly storms were predicted by evening.

Eileen, a friend Vicki grew up with, arrived to help with the inside recovery effort. Noticing that the inside workers had already filled many boxes and tubs; she insisted that we make immediate arrangements to rent storage for our growing cash of salvaged treasurers. She knew who to call and she took care of it.

Our daughters, one who lived in Seneca and the other who lived in Neosho, Missouri, arrived to assist. It was good to be surrounded by family. On an errand to Dollar General to get trash bags they noticed a sign advertising duplexes for rent. They jotted down the information. Returning to the house they called and made an appointment for us to view the property immediately.

This three bedroom duplex was just what we needed and the owner would even let us store stuff in the garage while his crew finished up some cosmetic items inside. It would be days before the duplex would have electricity. It would also be a while before we would have time to shop for furniture. We could appreciate the peace of knowing we had a place to go. This was a time when we relaxed and planned our next steps on our journey

Before we had time to ponder the housing offer, a representative from the insurance company was in our front yard. The agent from their storm

Bridging The Gap

recovery detail met with us and provided needed reassurance that things would be all right. He said we were fully covered for both the structure and its contents. We were also covered 100 % for out-of- pocket living expenses.

He briefly toured the structure and told us that it was his opinion that the house was a total loss, but stopped short of making it official. He said only an adjuster could make that declaration. He issued us a check for $8,000 and told us to find a hotel for the short term. He suggested that we make arrangements for long term housing as soon as possible. This was good news.

We told him of the offer for the duplex. He said that it was a reasonable offer and if it met with our approval we should sign a lease immediately. The owner brought the lease agreement by and we took a break from our clean up to sign it. With keys in hand, we were no longer homeless.

The temperature was on the rise and the humidity was making work difficult. It was still morning. Several times during the day volunteers came through the affected areas with snacks and drinks, water and Gatorade. As the noon hour approached the Salvation Army and the Red Cross offered meals at the clean-up sites.

These organizations were on the scene everyday providing assistance, snacks and meals. A disaster center was set up at the high school. FEMA representatives as well as counselors from the Red Cross were available for many days following the storm. Cleaning supplies and other item related to the recovery were available at the high school to those affected. The Salvation Army and the Red Cross assisted in preparing hot evening meals for workers and victims.

After a break for lunch that was delivered by volunteers, our crew turned their "eyes to the sky." Clouds were building and the winds were increasing and the earlier forecast of storms was becoming more likely. If we were going to continue to recover items we were going to have to make the house more secure. We were going to have to cover the windows and tarp the gaping holes in the roof.

Additional family and friends strengthened our recovery effort. My brother, his wife, and my son-in-law all joined in the recovery effort. My Aunt Betty, Sharon's mom, joined us on the second day. Tarps were acquired from the supplies at the high school. Caution and patience were required to stretch the tarps to close the roof openings. At least twice an unsteady step resulted in a temporary collapse, but the acrobatic volunteers managed to avoid serious injury. Pieces of plywood, siding and other debris were used to cover window openings.

With the house somewhat weatherproof, delivering recovered items to storage completed the first day activities. We used a trailer and a pickup truck to deliver item we would not need until we moved into a new house into storage units. Items we could use to set up housekeeping were delivered to the garage at the duplex.

As night fall approached we had to retreat and call it a day. After making decisions in regard to the next day, our recovery crew went their separate ways. While most of the volunteers that helped would be returning; for now we were all alone. For the first time since the storm we were alone; alone with each other and the memories of the past twenty-five years. We still had not seen even a sign of our cats. Silently we closed the front door and walked to our car. Lighting and muffled thunder filled in the darkness of the night.

Where were we going? We were still wearing the clothes we wore to church two days ago. As we approached the neighboring city it began to drizzle. We pulled into the first hotel we came to and were turned away as they were already sold out. It never occurred to me that I might not find a place to spend the night. The desk clerk quickly added that the hotel next door still had rooms. With that we quickly headed that way and checked in.

We agreed that we were not going to the room until we went to Wal-Mart. We needed clothes, underwear, socks, toiletries and other essentials before we could face another minute.

A relaxing shower and a good night's sleep was all the energy left for that day.

I lay waiting for sleep. I could hear the thunder and see the lightning flashing across the night sky. There were several periods of heavy rain during the night. That night, God took my anxiety, my worry, and my fear of the unknown on his shoulders and left me to quiet, peaceful sleep.

CHAPTER 19

COUNTDOWN TO TOMORROW

A busy eighteen days followed. Everything salvageable from the house had to be removed and placed in storage. We had to shop for furniture and other items and be ready to move into our new duplex. We also had to start planning for the mission trip.

Perhaps the most important thing to happen during that time was the visit from the insurance adjuster. He checked in on us a few days after our initial agent contact. When he arrived, we talked in the yard and he walked around the house. He took pictures to document the damage. The inside visit was brief. He declared the structure to be unsafe, and he declared it a total loss.

While it was sad to think that this house was destined for demolition, it helped us work through our current circumstances and helped us to plan for our future. He said it would take a few days to complete the claim but we should have our settlement in about a week. Then we should make arrangements to have the house demolished and the lot cleared.

The weather for this time period continued to be extremely hot and muggy. There was full sun every day. This made the kind of work we had to do difficult. While volunteers continued to provide us with ice, water and Gatorade; the possibility of dehydration and other heat related illnesses remained. At the end of each day we were physically and emotionally drained.

At church, the Sunday after the storm, I experienced what it means to be a member of the community of Christ. In church I felt that strength and power that comes from collective prayer. I also realized that some of my strength of the past week was the result of others' prayers. It was a great reassuring feeling. The power of prayer is real and the power of collective prayer is awesome.

During this initial recovery period we received food and other donations from numerous sources. SAM's Club, my wife's employer, and her fellow employees donate both food and money. We also received support for our teacher friends. Even though we were both retired, we still enjoyed the support of our continuing friends in education. We even received financial support from my Indian tribe, the Seneca-Cayuga Indian Tribe of Oklahoma.

It was hard at first to accept these gifts. We took great satisfaction in helping others but had ever been on the receiving end. We were thankful for all of those who supported us through the recovery process.

While the neighborhood looked torn apart, the people who made up the neighborhood became closer than ever. It was the general consensus that people would remain in the neighborhood because they wouldn't want to live anywhere else. We were there for each other for the long haul.

By the end of the first week the electric company had restored power to some parts of town and we understood that we would have power at the duplex on the following Monday. That meant we would have to take time from our packing and look toward furnishing are new place. By Saturday evening we had purchased the needed pieces of furniture and they were scheduled to be delivered on Monday.

Monday arrived, our new furnishings arrived and we slept in our new place for the first night. That day we also hired a crew to move our refrigerator and other big items including my piano. The remainder of the day was spent cleaning the new area, filling cupboards and stocking up on food. Meals and snacks were still available while we were working during the day but we provide for ourselves at breakfast and dinner.

We continued to work at the old place. With each passing day we came closer and closer to being able to say good-by. We were spending more and more time at our new place trying to address our current needs and looking forward. We began thinking about the mission trip. We were able to spend time with Little Calvin again. He was probably the most therapeutic part of our recovery chapter.

Our cats, which are like family members, began to appear. As we worked through our days of cleaning and salvaging, they appeared; one at a time. One came from a closet, another through the exposed studs, and one was just waiting in the front room. We left out food and water. On the day we planned to vacate the house permanently, we were still missing "Grey Kitty."

The weather took a turn. This day started out damp and drizzly. It was much cooler than other days. Vicki had gotten up earlier than usual. I really didn't know she had left the house. When I realized she was gone I was somewhat concerned but neither of us had been acting "normal" since the storm.

Before long I heard the door open and out of the rain came my wife carrying that Grey cat. Vicki said she was lying in bed and just felt the need to seek out that cat one last time. When she arrived at the house, there she was waiting to be rescued.

With the acquisition of that cat we were ready to say good-by. We went over to the house later in the day for one more walk through and then we left and closed the door behind us. It was a quiet, tearful walk to the car. I can only speak for myself, but a lot of memories were streaming through my mind as we drove away for the last time.

CHAPTER 20

LEAP OF FAITH

Only five weeks ago I sat in the solitude of my church and ask God to take hold of my life and show me the way. Just a few hours ago I left my house for demolition.

There I was standing with my wife on a church parking lot in the middle of the night, ready to board a southbound bus. Our destination was Mexico; our mission was to save souls.

Vicki and I were still in the "walking wounded" category from the tornado. We had thrown our work clothes in a bag and were awaiting our turn to board. We looked like refugees, we were tired and weary but we were surrounded by a strong community of faith.

Vicki and I were in a sense, strangers. Even though we were with our friends Ida and Richard I was still a bit uneasy. It was a requirement to go on the mission trip that you be prepared to discuss your conversion experience. Being Episcopalian I was a bit weak in the witnessing department. I suppose that they prayed for us, and let us come along anyway.

Following a prayer, we boarded the bus for the night time portion of our journey. While space was limited and my quarters were restricted to a single bus seat, I settled in for the night. As the bus pulled out of the church parking lot and made its way through town I remember simply asking God for the strength to do his will.

Once again God was there holding me up. He replaced my anxious moments of the unknown with a peaceful promise of safety and love.

As the bus roared through the night, there was some soft, spiritual singing and clapping but in a very short time the "rhythm of the road," gave way to peaceful rest.

This was a peaceful rest that was a long time coming. Since the evening of the tornado we experienced sleep from exhaustion and always awoke to the seemingly endless disaster.

The next morning I was greeted by a happy and warm glow from the sun and a Ranger Cookie. I soon learned that Ranger Cookies were a unique selection of ingredients blended into an oatmeal cookie batter. They appeared to be a staple in the sustenance for those in the mission field.

The day that dawned was remarkable. The morning light supported a communion of faith. I could feel the energy. The electricity of the moment was miraculous. The atmosphere reflected feelings of sharing, caring, and bonding.

The make-up of our mission group was very diverse. There were professional people as well as retail clerks and burger flippers. There were married couples and single men and women. Many in this group were retired, but some were college students still looking for their life's calling. Some required special needs. To many, this was not their first mission experience.

While the mission trip represented a common objective, almost every participant had a personal goal which they hoped to achieve. The diversity of the group also brought a diversity of talents. All of us were bound together with "Christian Love.

Our destination was a church camp in south Texas near the Mexican border. We enjoyed clean, adequate dormitory accommodations. Our meals were supplied by a dining hall. The grounds of the camp provided a natural, spiritual landscape for fellowship and reflection.

We were required to travel light as every bit of additional space on the bus was reserved for mission supplies. Behind the bus we pulled a covered trailer filled with clothing, school supplies, material and other items needed by those our mission would serve.

In addition we carried with us medical supplies to be used in on-site health clinics, sewing machines and sewing supplies to be used by the women of the village we were serving, and tools needed to continue the construction project initiated the previous year. Loads of lumber and other building materials had already been collected and delivered to the village site inside Mexico.

On our arrival at the camp, we set out our bedding and then began to sort those supplies we carried with us. Our mission director lived in South Texas and worked closely with the mission ministries and those in Mexico. We delivered some of our supplies to his home where he had onsite space to store items we may not be able to transport across the border during our stay.

The remainder of the first evening was spent settling in and getting to know each other. The men and women were separated so the women had additional time to interact with each other as did the men. There was a large meeting room joining the two dorm areas. As we gathered that first evening the anxiety associated with personal testimony again presented itself.

The time we had already spent together made sharing easy and by bedtime of the first evening we had focused all of our individual energy into one unified cause. In the week that would pass we would learn of each person's talent and learn to appreciate how all of our individual offerings can cause great things to happen.

The next morning we were introduced to the village that would be the primary source of our mission work. It was a small village hugging the border just across from the U.S. city of Brownsville.

The natives of the village were poor but proud. They were caring individuals who were willing to share what little they had. Unemployment in the village was high. The job offerings were mostly manual labor. A prison for men was located nearby. Many of the village inhabitants were wives of prisoners. They were trying to earn enough money to pay for their loved ones in prison and still have enough to raise their families. The young people of the village did have a school.

When we returned to camp after that first day there was a message on our voice mail that our tornado ravaged home had been demolished and the ground cleared. I must admit that it was an emotional moment, and I shed a tear, but I understood that it was part of the process necessary for us to get on with our life.

The primary source of our mission was a small village Baptist church, supported by the mission group we were representing. Construction of this church was a multi-year project of the mission alliance. While this construction project was a year round endeavor, one of the goals of our week long mission experience was to construct wooden pews for the church. Many on the men were involved in this construction project.

Because I was a trained educator, I worked with a group responsible for providing a bible school for the area youth. In addition to relating stories about the teachings of Jesus we also provided needed school supplies for the community youth. While lacking adequate language training provided a challenge, I could feel the difference that we made in the lives of those young people we served.

One of my main duties on this adventure was to document our accomplishments with pictures. Through the camera lens I recorded examples of poverty, pain, and suffering. Through the facial expressions I recorded instances of hope and happiness. Through the eyes of the natives you could see souls supported by faith.

While much of our time was spent at the village church, our mission group also offered onsite clinics for families in need. Some of our mission workers spent time with village women providing them with sewing machines and sewing supplies and instruction on how to use sewing skills to provide income for their families.

A particularly spiritual part of every day was when we crossed the border. We were always travelling with vans full of volunteers and supplies. The truth is on some occasions we were transporting items across the border that that the Mexican government could considered not appropriate. Had they discovered these items they could have been confiscated and we could have been detained and not allowed to enter the country. Each day we would stop just shy of the border and say a prayer for our safe passage. On more than one day the border patrol searched our vehicles but we were allowed through on each occasion.

Another very spiritual moment came when we took a trip to the City Dump. It is a sad but true fact that the poor of the city pay for the right to go through the trash at the dump. As we drove through the sky-high piles of garbage we would stop and pass out prepared bags of survival items and scripture offerings to those in need.

On lady had no shoes and had cuts on her feet. Vicki was so moved by this women's situation that she took off her shoes and gave them away in hopes that this person's life might be a little easier. An example of how God moves in our lives.

At night we slept from exhaustion, but we awoke each morning with a renewed faith that the day's work would provide hope for those in need.

The lesson I learned is "when you sign up to serve God, you are signing up to do it his way." My only problem in the early parts of this experience was that I felt I knew a better way. When I overcame my desire to be in charge and allowed myself to be his servant; I began to enjoy all the rewards of being a messenger of faith.

After spending a week with this strong community of faith Vicki and I returned home ready to move forward. When we visited our old home site, the house was gone and the ground was clear. We felt better. The cleared ground was a sign that the bad was gone and it was time to look to the future.

CHAPTER 21

ONE MORE TRIP

I returned home from the Mexico trip late on a Saturday night. Two days later I was standing on a school parking lot in the middle of the night waiting to jump on a bus for a different type of mission trip. It was 4:00 A.M. and this group of eighth and ninth graders was waiting to board the bus for a ten day adventure to our nation's east coast.

The trip was offered by the school's history department as an elective to study historical sites that laid the ground work for a nation's history. Because the last month of classes had been canceled after the tornado destroyed the district's schools, there were those who felt it best to cancel the trip. After polling those affected by the storm administrators felt that both parents and students were all in favor of proceeding with it as planned.

As the students and adult sponsors stepped aboard the charter coach I could tell the mood of this group was different. Because of the darkness I could not see facial expressions but interaction was minimal. With this age group you never experience long periods of minimal interaction even in the middle of the night.

Because of the extreme circumstances surrounding this event, a prayer for safe travel was offered and the bus pulled out into the darkness.

That "rhythm of the road" again reigned supreme and in just a short time all were enjoying comfortable, restful sleep. I remembered that first night on the mission trip and I realized that many of the participants in this activity were among the "tornado's walking wounded."

That is when I realized that survival was the theme for many of these youngsters. History was going to be secondary, this time. Thus, I label this adventure a mission trip.

With the morning sun and our breakfast stop students began an almost immediate bonding process. Many of those traveling with us opened their eyes for the first time in a month and did not see or feel the overwhelming depression of the tornado's destruction. Several of our young travelers had lost everything and were living in local hotel/motels. Others were living in homes that were badly damaged. For all of those affected this journey had to offer some type of relief.

The first day was pretty much a travel day and as the bus cruised down the interstate the bonding process continued. Many of our travelers were good friends but hadn't even talked to each other since the storm. Most did not realize the predicaments of their fellow classmates. Students began to gather themselves into small group and assess the personal situations of their traveling companions. The senses of these students seemed dulled while their emotion seemed heightened.

As the days passed our rolling therapy session continued to make strides. Students who never realized they could be good listeners and others who never felt qualified to offer advice on personal growth or guidance all stepped up. Our adults who also were divided between those affected by the storm and those not just added to the human dimension of hurt and healing. God was present on that bus and with no formal presentation our traveling participants had developed into a community of faith.

Rooming with four students allowed me an opportunity to be a good shepherd to those in need. I always took advantage of these opportunities to present myself and my spiritual story. This year I felt my personal testimony was only supplementing belief systems that many of these youngsters had recently recharged on their own.

This trip offered a number of faith related sites. It presented several opportunities to defend the idea of "one nation under God," and the idea of "God and Country." When I started traveling with this group, they visited sites like Gettysburg and Valley Forge but presented it to the students in a rather sterile manner, emphasizing strictly the historical facts. This textbook style of presentation left a void when it came to the total picture.

I am proud to say that I am somewhat responsible for the opportunity that those students had to explore the ideas of linking hope and faith with the idea of courage and surviving. It allowed our traveling youngster an understanding that a "Faith in God" was an important quality that Heroes are made of.

Several years after I began working with this program I begged that the trip leader include Christ's Church in Philadelphia on our list of sites. After a couple of years of whining, he scheduled a tour. The presenter at Christ Church did such a good job of making the connection to a "Faith in God," and the success of "our founding fathers," that it just naturally became the element that completed the historical picture. Later, on that same trip, the National Cathedral became a destination point. Since that year, God got due credit for his role in creating this great nation.

With many of our young traveler's enhanced understanding of hope and faith and for their need to survive, it was easy for them to relate the faith and hope that was necessary at sites like Gettysburg and Valley Forge. It was easy for them to understand the commitment and courage it took to plan and stage a revolution. How could our founding fathers proceed without a "Faith in God?"

The Holocaust Museum presented faith in perhaps the most critical of circumstances. You actually experienced "Faith" as you set quietly in the Museums Hall of Reflection at the end of your tour. After this visit our travelers were able to better understand Judaism and were able to put faces of sacrifice on their Jewish friends and instructors.

The group experienced intense spirituality at the Vietnam War Memorial and at Arlington National Cemetery. These sites also offered strong emotions of faith at the greatest level, the level that involved sacrifice. It was at the World War II Memorial where our student travelers were able to interact with survivors who were excited to share their stories of courage and sacrifice. Those students got to shake the hands of living American Heroes.

As we left the capitol city we travelled south to Williamsburg, Virginia for historic stops at Jamestown and Colonial Williamsburg. Maybe more important than history was that this stay-over included two opportunities for some time to relax and enjoy each other.

A trip to Virginia Beach to enjoy the ocean and a visit to Busch Garden's Amusement Park gave our storm weary travelers a chance to have fun and fellowship with their bus buddies before heading home to the unknown.

After two days of R & R we headed home. We enjoyed one more historic site at Charlottesville, Virginia where we visited Thomas Jefferson's Monticello. Then, we travelled through some of the most beautiful reflective, scenery in America as we motored across West Virginia. John Denver said it all in his hit song "Take Me Home Country Road."

Our journey was quickly drawing to a close. For me that means at some point I must face the fact that there are things that are going to have to be done on my return. It is easy to get overcome from all that lies ahead.

For our travelers it's a return to normal. But what is normal? It's back to better. It's back to a future. A future that can better be understood and accepted by these youngsters as they return to their evolving existence. Their time on the road hopefully resulted in a better understanding of ideas like faith and hope.

For me I was as vulnerable as anyone on the trip, but travelling with these resilient youngsters made me more hopeful. I saw eighth and ninth graders change right before my eyes. It was not because of anything I did. I was a part of the change. We all returned home to some uncertainty and fear of the unknown, but our journey made this homecoming one of confidence and optimism.

OUR MISSION WAS ACCOMPLISHED!

CHAPTER 22

CHANGING DIRECTION

The junior high school trip started out as cloudy for me as it was for the students. When I awoke from my first sleep on the bus I felt alone and a little guilty. The person who I had shared those times of uncertainty with was no longer by my side. I longed for Vicki and I felt guilty that I had abandoned her.

It wasn't long until I realized that everyone on that bus was having the same feelings and we were placed together on this occasion to help each other. We all used our cell phones to get our reassurances from home that allowed us to enjoy what was happening in our lives. The resilient young people proved to be good medicine for us all.

On returning home Vicki and I discovered that the period had been a time of reflection for us both. We were now ready to work together again as we planned for the next portion of our life. The primary step in this transition was to plan and build a new home.

Building a new house at our age was not as easy or as fun as it may sound. We had raised our family and were content to enjoy our daughters and their families in the house we already had.

As one of our relatives who just lived a block away and who also lost her home put it, "I built one home in my life and I just don't feel like I can do that again."

She was looking at her home and her family as one. I could understand how she felt, but we proceeded to take the next step and started to look at houses and floor plans and deciding what we felt would meet our current needs.

Vicki's father Leroy had been a builder and volunteered to draw our house plans. We graciously accepted his offer. That way we didn't have to build one of the houses from a book and we could include some features that personalized our place.

In the midst of our planning, my daughter Rebecca announced that Little Calvin was going to have a little brother around the first of the year. That translated into a need for a room for the boys when they came to spend the night and additional space for toys and play. News of a baby is always exciting especially if you are a grandparent.

It was about this time that we finalized our house plans and were ready to begin construction. While the thought of starting over seemed ominous, after working through the floor plans we were ready to begin this project.

But not so fast!

When our builder went to the city to file for a building permit we found that new construction codes and the fact that we had a corner lot required that we had set back regulations on two sides. The house as it was drawn wouldn't fit on the lot.

So we went back to the drawing board, literally. Leroy was OK with changing the plan. His biggest concern was our happiness. Fathers are like that. One proposal that would allow us to keep the same plan required us to change the direction of the house which would change our address and our view. We were about to settle on that just so we could get started.

Leroy knew we were not happy and offered some new plan designs that would still encompass our major wants. We settled on one of those new designs. After acquiring our building permit we began construction in late September.

The long wait began. I did some substitute teaching, mainly to help the time pass. As the holidays approached our anxiety switched from house to baby. By the first of December a skeleton of our home was rising out of the destruction but as we celebrated Christmas waiting for baby was heavy on our mind.

When the phone rang two days after Christmas announcing that baby was on the way, we were surprised. While we were tired of waiting we really hadn't considered a baby quite yet. We dropped everything and raced to the hospital. Later in the day, on December 27th, Wilson Davis Depriest was born. I'm proud to say that I negotiated the name, Wilson, Vicki's family name, and Davis, Brett's mother's family name.

After the first of the year all attention was on the building project. With the winter months building opportunities were hampered. Warm days in March allowed for a pick-up in the pace. It was the week before Easter that we started moving in. We hosted the family Easter dinner. Ironically it was almost a year since I had asked God to give my family a new beginning and that Easter Sunday marked completion of the physical marker of that change.

The summer of 2004 was busy as we worked on landscaping. Our goal was to change the black mud into green spaces. We also planted trees and shrubs and completed our project by raising a flag pole in the horseshoe of the circle drive. To mark the finish of the rebuild I hung a picture in the entry way showing the old house and the new as a reminder of where we came from and where we were going.

During the fall of 2004 I began some serious substituting. Most of my time was spent in the elementary and middle grade in my hometown and in neighboring communities. My reason for working was to earn extra money. Grandparents always need extra money. I always enjoyed working with kids and I must admit that working with the younger kids was fun. Try as I did, it was difficult to feel any kind of satisfaction except for surviving the day. I worked fairly steady for the remainder of 2004.

The year wound down with the holidays. This year we had two little ones to help us celebrate Thanksgiving and Christmas. It had been a rough 18 months since the tornado but God had blessed us with a new grandchild and a new house and for those things we were deeply grateful.

CHAPTER 23

LOSING SIGHT

The time just before Christmas was extremely busy. In addition to all the holiday activities I had agreed to work several days at a satellite school for troubled youth. I was driving about 10 miles a day to get to my assignment. This time of the year, the early morning sun was bright and directly in my eyes for the entire drive. Seeing the road was extremely difficult. The angle of the early evening sun in December made the drive home equally challenging.

Even when I was not driving, it seemed that my senses were heightened to bright light. Images seemed to blend into the brightness. On the way home the day the schools dismissed for Christmas I stopped at Walmart. While shopping I passed right in front of my father-in-law and Joan and when I looked right at them and didn't speak, they teasingly accused me of being a snob or just ignoring them. I saw their outline but I realized that I really didn't recognize them.

My sight continued to deteriorate, but it was Christmas and I simply didn't have time to do anything. What eye doctor was going to have an opening three days before Christmas?

Bridging The Gap

While I was working, I blamed the bright sensation on my drive to and from school on the sun, but now I was home most of the day and I was noticing that I was having trouble seeing television. Everything seemed to be blurry. I had prescription glasses but they provided no relief. Everything was washed out by the light.

Christmas Day came and the family gathered. After dinner we opened presents. The boys received one of their favorite gifts, books. We started reading to our grandchildren while they were still in the hospital.

Little Wil climbed up on Pappy's lap toting a new book. He wasn't talking but everyone in the room knew he wanted me to read it to him. With tears in my eyes I deferred to Nanny.

To those present it just looked like I didn't want to do it. I felt terrible because I couldn't see the words. At that point I realized that something serious was happening to my vision. But it was Christmas. I didn't want to cause alarm and ruin the holiday. Whatever the problem, it could wait until tomorrow.

The day after Christmas was one of the most demanding, busy days in the retail world and Vicki was scheduled to work until 8:00 p.m. We were also actively preparing for Little Wil's first birthday. I spent the day at home fidgeting around and getting more worked up by the minute. I spent a great deal of the day on the computer researching eye conditions. As you would guess, serious was attached to any ailment interfering with your vision.

I had a couple of friends that had recently suffered detached retinas and my symptom seemed similar. After internet research I was sure that was what was going on in my head. Of course, treatment needed to begin immediately. As I waited for Vicki to get off work my anxiety was rising. By the time she got home I was having trouble seeing anything.

As soon as Vicki retuned home I declared that I needed to go to the emergency room. I explained to her that I thought I was suffering from a detached retina. If that was the case, the sooner I was treated the better the chances of saving my vision. I was ready and we left for the ER.

It was a slow night at the hospital so we got into an exam room right away. They dimmed the light while I waited for the doctor. My vital signs appeared to be normal but even the light in the exam room was washing away clarity When the doctor arrived he asked what was going on.

I explained my symptoms and told him that I thought I might have a detached retina. After a close eye exam, the ER physician reported that it was not a detached retina.

If it was not a detached retina, then what was it?

The exam revealed swelling and an apparent infection in one eye. A vision check using the eye chart on the wall proved my vision was bad, maybe even legally blind. The hospital doctor set up an appointment with an eye specialist for early the next morning. The ER physician highly recommended this doctor and said I was lucky that he was the on call doctor that night. Otherwise I might have waited a long time to get an appointment.

It was the middle of the night before we got home. There was nothing especially alarming about the ER visit except the use of the word blind. Then there were, of course, those internet tags of serious that accompanied all abnormalities of the eye.

Lying in bed that night, staring into the darkness I remember hoping that my vision loss could be halted. I wasn't even asking for improvements, just no more loss. I realized in that early morning reflection that I was not only losing sight in reference to vision, but I was also losing sight, in a larger way, in my faith. I immediately turned my wishes into prayers. My anxiety was suspended and I slept peacefully.

The morning brought on a day of confusion. I had a morning appointment with an eye specialist, and I had Little Wil's first birthday celebration in the evening. What happened in the middle and how I got from one event to another was a mystery. It was one full day.

Vicki and I arrived at the office of the eye specialist, registered and filled out all of the paper work afforded a new patient. A series of routine test followed. After the vision test I met with the doctor. He confirmed that I was in deed legally blind in one eye and close to that status in the other. His mission was to find out why I was experiencing the current symptoms, why I was experiencing the vision loss, and could the loss be stopped and possibly reversed.

The preliminary tests revealed trauma in one eye and some unknown infection that was affecting both eyes. Further testing showed extreme pressure on the optic nerve and a possible blockage to the optic nerve.

The doctor felt that he needed more information before making a diagnosis. He prescribed an anti-inflammatory for the swelling and an antibiotic to combat the unknown infection. I was also to report immediately to the hospital lab for important blood work that needed to be reported to the doctor's office immediately. If it tested positive I would need to begin a medication immediately to prevent further vision loss. He also scheduled an appointment for me with a reputable neurologist.

By now it was midafternoon and Wil's party was still ahead. We reported to the lab for the blood work. I requested the results by sent to the doctor. I had prescriptions to fill to counter the infections. I was to return to the eye doctor after the first of the year.

Then it was on to Wal-Mart. I was on a schedule. We had a party to get ready for. While the pharmacy worked on filling my prescriptions we did our shopping for the party. It was now late afternoon and our party guests would be arriving in about two hours.

That was a wild day and the first of many to come. We waited anxiously for a call from the doctor to report on the one blood test. A positive finding would require another trip to the pharmacy. The call never came and our day of mystery came to an end.

The next eye appointment was brief. The doctor went over the blood work. He explained that I was not suffering from the sight stealing eye disease. His exam also indicated that the swelling was retreating and the pressure on the optic should be relieved. This pattern of improvement could signal a vision improvement, but on this day it remained the same. My next appointment would be after my visit to the neurologist.

The visit to the neurologist was next. The two week wait had allowed my anxiety level to escalate. While it is true that the report from the eye specialist showed improvement, the word "blockage" remained in my memory. After the routine business of a first time visit, I set down to visit about my condition. Even with the improved report from the eye specialist, this doctor was concerned about what triggered the incident. He felt that there were a number of conditions that could trigger my symptoms. My incident could be an early sign of MS, MD, or it could be related to a brain tumor.

There was that word. The one I have been obsessing over since the eye doctor first mentioned a possible blockage. Now it was a possibility.

To rule out each of these serious situations he prescribed a number of tests. The two most defining tests were an MRI of the brain, and a spinal tap. A spinal tap is often used to confirm meningitis. That's another scary thought. He also wanted a complete blood work-up.

The MRI was scheduled at the hospital for the following Monday morning with the lab work to follow that afternoon. The spinal tap was scheduled for that Thursday in the doctor's office. As Vicki and I left that appointment all I could think about was that word "tumor."

That night as I wrestled with the day's events, I had another one of those "fatherly" talks about my shaken faith. My feelings were that I must find out my medical situation, accept it and learn to live with it. I would adjust. I would live.

Gods answer, "I'll never give you more than you can handle." The word tumor alone is far from fatal.

The MRI and the lab work were routine tests and went as planned. The spinal tap was not that simple. Anytime someone prefaces a procedure with, "during this procedure you will experience a minimal discomfort," be cautious. After that day, I wondered what major discomfort would be like.

After three failed attempts in the doctor's office, he referred me to the hospital to have the test completed. Three failed attempts equaled three stabs in the lower back with a long sharp needle. I was not excited at the prospect of even one more attempt.

Vicki was there to comfort me and as always restore my confidence.

A few hours had passed since the office failures but the area of testing was still tender. The numbing substance they applied prior to the procedure was not effective and I knew I just had to bite the bullet and get it over with. After two tries at the hospital I was really ready to just walk away. The lab crew begged me to stay for one more try. If that was unsuccessful, they would schedule the test as an out-patient surgery and I would be put to sleep for the procedure. The third time was a charm. The final poke was just as painful as the five preceding ones, but this time it was over.

That earlier "walk away" comment was really not a probability as it was several days before I could walk in a normal fashion, side effects from all that poking and probing.

Despite the negativity associated with this procedure I did receive some encouraging news. As I was leaving one of the techs commented, "Did they do an MRI on your brain."

I explained that they had done that test on Monday.

The tech replied, "That's good, then you can rule out a tumor. They would have called back the same day if there was any sign of a tumor."

Did I hear right? Was there no tumor? This was not a doctor's report but it was good enough for me.

My doctor's visit the next week confirmed my no tumor status. He also reported that the tests for all of the debilitating conditions came back negative. On my return to the eye doctor, he reported that the swelling was gone, there was no apparent infection and my vision was as good as I could expect. This whole experience had been long and scary. The main results, I was not suffering from a horrible disease, and my strong faith had again carried me through.

My next conversation with God was one of thanks and one of reaffirmation. Having been delivered from this crisis, I knew that there was more to my journey. It was about to make another major turn.

CHAPTER 24

TURN AROUND RANCH

The thoughts of tumors and lost vision made me realize what a blessing my life is. I was sure that my spiritual journey was about to take a turn, I just had to be aware and not miss it.

Just before the Christmas break I worked at a satellite school for troubled youth. It was a boarding school for student who had troubled backgrounds. Many were wards of the court. Some were involved in abusive situations, some were victims.

The organization is known as Turn Around Ranch. It is resident facility operated by a local mental health provider. The educational service for the facility is provided by the local school district. The case load at the facility was co-ed and the student's ranged in age from 10 to 18. The curriculum was very structured, class sizes were small and the students were ability grouped.

The classes were limited to ten students. Each classroom was assigned a teacher and a teaching assistance. Along with state approved curriculum the staff at the school worked extra hard to provide a positive environment for learning.

There was also a focus on developing and practicing social skills. Students were constantly presented with the idea that decisions result in consequences, good decisions render good consequences and bad decisions result in bad ones.

My school experiences since I retired were no more than working as a substitute, one day and then another, with my only satisfaction being finishing each day and getting paid. When the phone rang early in the morning requesting that I substitute, I made a decision based strictly on how I felt about working that day. I had little loyalty to substituting; the only satisfaction was surviving.

Things were different at Turn Around Ranch. The first day I worked there I felt the appreciation of those students. They had been to hell and back and they looked on the time I was spending with them as quality time. They knew there were worse places they could be. While many had personal issues, this environment allowed for time for the students to work through them. It was the best model for working with troubled students that I had ever worked with during my public school career. I felt great satisfaction for my work at Turn Around Ranch from the very beginning.

I welcomed calls from the ranch and felt an immediate loyalty to it. I could never say no. The kids at the ranch appreciated what all the adults at the facility had to offer. They appreciated the fact that you were there. They knew that you took an interest in their well-being. They sensed your nonjudgmental attitude and they knew that you could accept them for what they were. They knew that you cared.

I liked working at the ranch and welcomed any opportunity to serve there. I felt that I again could make a difference even if I only worked one day a week. I worked almost exclusively there after my loss of vision episode.

During the month of March I accepted an assignment to work every day. I could have worked the remainder of the year but I had made a commitment earlier to work the last nine weeks of the school years at another community school.

I was disappointed that I could not finish the year at the ranch, but felt the necessity to honor my prior commitment. What I gained from my work at the ranch was confidence that I could still make a difference in the life of a child. That was the deal that I made with God so many years ago. For the first time since retirement I felt needed and satisfied that my life was making a difference.

While my assignment to close out the year was steady work I was still just a substitute filling in for a teacher that dearly loved her students and her students dearly loved her.

In the beginning it was a survival game, but I was there long enough to inject my enthusiasm and teaching style into the daily plan. I was still challenged by the loyal supporters of the classroom teacher but as the days passed I did feel I was "making a difference." Did I get the opportunity to tell my story? I never pass up an opportunity to share with young people. Nine weeks is a short time to establish trust, but there were students who took value from my teaching.

The last day of school I collected the books, turned in my grades and walked out the door, my commitment fulfilled. I accepted an invitation to join the staff for dinner and I enjoyed the camaraderie of a group of educators again. It felt good to be a part of a team if only for the remainder of that day.

I returned home to my retired status but with a good pay check. Vicki and I were enjoying our new home especially when the grand-boys spent the night. But the summer was long and I had spent the last fifteen weeks with heightened stimulation and daily activity. I had regained my confidence to educate at Turn Around Ranch, and I developed a certainty that I could get up and go to work on a routine basis from my end of the year experience.

God was laying out that turn in the road and I was going to follow it and see where it led me.

CHAPTER 25

ON THE ROAD AGAIN

Throughout the summer months I began to explore the idea of going back to work on an everyday basis. Because I was receiving a state pension, there were rules that applied. If I worked for any school district in the state of Missouri I would be limited to no more than half time employment. Opportunities to work on a more full time basis were possible if I took a job out of state, or if I worked for a private or parochial school system. I was reading the want ads on a regular basis. I felt there was something for me, but I had to take care to locate it.

On a Sunday late in July, I was reading the local newspaper before church and I noticed an opening for a computer program coordinator at the local parochial high school. It was just part time, but it sounded interesting. It would be working in a high school, the only group of students I hadn't worked with, but I felt it was worth considering.

During church I realized that this might be the position I was waiting for. I prayed about the position and was amazed at how anxious I was to inquire about it. After church I discussed it with Vicki. With the two grand-boys we anticipated more opportunities to babysit. That was really the only thing keeping me from applying. Vicki's response was that she didn't care, if I wanted to go back to work I should. She said she just didn't want me to be disappointed if I wasn't selected.

Later that night I reread the ad. There was no application process. All I needed to do was send my resume to the development office for the school system.

My next dilemma was writing a resume. I had never had to apply for any of my previous position and I had never developed a resume. I called my daughter Sarah and she talked me through the necessary points to resume writing. That Sunday evening I developed by first ever resume. The next day I reviewed it and tweaked it and faxed it to the school. Since I had no experience working with high school students, I was not really expecting to receive a call back.

Wednesday of that week Vicki and I treated ourselves to a trip Silver Dollar City. While visiting the amusement park attractions I received a call on my cell phone from the development director about the job. He said he had received my resume and wanted me to come in later in the day for an interview. I explained that I was currently out of town but I could come in the next morning.

I couldn't help but feel the irony of this situation. It was Silver Dollar City that almost cost me my life and set me on this lifetime journey of service, and now this position could afford me the opportunity to continue that journey.

When I told my wife about my phone conversation, her response was, "I thought you decided not to apply for that position." I thought at first that she was disappointed, but realized soon that she was as always my number one supporter.

The interview was short and to the point. First, the position involved over-seeing an online learning program. The training would be a part of the position. The job was for thirty hours a week. The development director was more interested in my knowledge of computers and how I could work with people than he was about my lack of experience with high school students.

He continued by holding up a large stack of papers and commented that he had read more than forty resumes and none were close to what he had in mind. He told me that I had all the qualifications. If I was still interested the job was mine.

My instinct was to accept his offer at that time but just two days before I read an article in the AARP Journal that suggested that you wait at least twenty-four hours before you accept an offer. I asked if I could have a day to think it over. He said I could call him tomorrow before 3:00 p.m. He was going to Las Vegas and said he hoped to fill this position before he left town.

I called early the next morning accepted the job and told him to have fun in Vegas. He thanked me and said he would see me the third week in August.

* * * * *

Weeks after I was hired the administrative assistant in the development office told the story of how I was hired. She said that the job had been advertised for several weeks. He had received over forty resume to review and not one came close to filling his need. He had worked very hard in writing a grant to fund this position and was getting very depressed that he could not find anybody to fill it. The AA told him to pray about it and stop worrying. God would take it from there. The next morning when he came to work your resume was on the fax machine. He told me that God had sent him the perfect candidate.

* * * * *

My first appearance as a new employee was at the faculty back to school breakfast. The night before the meeting I was asked to talk to the group about what I would be doing.

I related to the group the information I had been given by the program developers. I then explained how the program could benefit students with special needs, students who had classes they needed to retake, and students who could not get the classes they needed because of scheduling conflicts.

I felt good ushering in a new program that could make a difference. That's what I was all about.

At the end of the meeting teachers from all grade levels introduced themselves and welcomed me into the system. One student's name kept coming up in our conversations. It was like the program was developed to meet the special needs of this student. God had sent me a challenge and school hadn't even started. I was still waiting to be trained.

The first few days of class were chaotic. All of my students had be enrolled and I had to develop an individual lesson plan for each of them. This process took about a week. It was not until the second week that I actually began to learn about my students. Because each of these first year students had a special need, the getting acquainted session was of real importance.

Seth, the name I kept hearing about over and over was enrolled in two of my classes. He had a personality to immediately make him popular and he was well liked by his classmates. He was also a favorite of the staff. Despite his strong personality and a sincere desire to learn, he was failing.

As we became acquainted it became obvious that he was extremely dyslexic, but very interested in learning. As we worked together I learned that he was a very good listener and a very observant visual learner. He spoke a very advanced vocabulary. He was a competent note taker, but only for his own eyes to read. He could read but it was very difficult and time consuming. He was a very capable young man with a disability.

Attending school was difficult for Seth. He was living with his sister and his father who was on disability from an automobile accident. His mother was working a job away from home but did provide as much support for the family as possible. Seth had to work, sometimes late at night, to help pay the bills. Even with the challenges at home he still came to school regularly and had a positive, cheerful attitude.

As I became settled into my position I found myself with a lot of free time. I invested a great deal of that time with Seth. His energy and his strong desire to learn made him the prime candidate for this new online adventure.

Because of his disability reading was a major hurdle towards his academic success. Seth could perform math activities with a degree of confidence, especially when time was not an issue. Language Arts and the content subjects provided a different kind of challenge. He was much more successful when he had assistance with reading.

Seth was also a very dedicated individual. Aside from his educational activities, he was a very proficient student in the culinary arts at the local tech center. He volunteered for before and after school learning opportunities to insure his success in his computer classes. At mid-term he was accelerating in the courses he was taking from me. We were both very proud.

Not long after that I was called to the office. When I entered Seth was there with the principal and the counselor. I may have failed to mention that Seth was a senior. The report from the counselor was extremely troubling.

A review of Seth's transcript revealed four years of hard work and almost no credit. The purpose of this meeting was to discuss Seth's future. In the beginning it was the general consensus that it would be impossible for him to graduate with his class. When I walked in Seth had a tear stained face, and I felt completely blindsided. Just days ago Seth and I were feeling victorious and now we both felt like failures.

My renewed confidence in making a difference was getting trampled on. I slipped in a quick prayer for direction. "Show me the way, Lord." Give me some direction," I asked? Then I heard these words come from my mouth. "Let's not give up, let's see if my program can help."

Did those words come out of my mouth? The only person in the room that showed any confidence in this plan was Seth. I believe I actually saw a non-verbal head shake from the principal and the counselor just tapped his pencil and agreed we would work together on the transcript and see if anything could be done.

After my meeting with the counselor the situation was still desperate. He needed nine additional classes to make up in addition to the classes he was enrolled in now. It was the beginning of October. That meant he had from now until the first of May to finish if he wanted to walk with his class. The counselor was doubtful but he, like everyone in the school, wanted Seth to be successful. He scheduled another meeting for the next morning.

As we gathered I was given the opportunity to explain how all of this was going to work. Work is the key word. The good news is he was going to finish the first semester in both of his current classes and would be able to complete them completely before Thanksgiving.

My question to Seth was, "Do you really want to graduate?"

By now tears were again streaming down his face.

The deal offered him the opportunity to graduate in May if he passed all the classes he was enrolled in currently and if he completed the remaining classes on the computer. We all acknowledged that this was a long shot and a lot would depend on his desire to finish. He couldn't afford a single set back.

I next asked, "Seth what can we expect from you if you try your hardest and still don't finish? Will you continue your intentions to receive a diploma or will you most likely drop out?"

I felt these were both relevant questions because if he was just going to drop out, why should he work his tail-off when the odds are stacked so high against him. Was his desire to walk with his class driven strictly for social motives?

He was quick to reply that he would go to summer school, and would return in the fall if necessary. He clarified that he had no intentions of dropping out."

I expressed my joy in his decision. It was agreed that the counselor would work closely with Seth and that he would monitor his progress in both his classroom work and his work on the computer. As the meeting broke up I told Seth that as long as he remained dedicated to his mission I would be beside him to help.

I then offered him a strong handshake. I remember that memorable handshake I received from my doctor after the accident and how it dictated confidence and trust between us and I hoped that those same feeling were transmitted in my handshake.

Seth added to his intent by continuing his before and after school visits and also showed up during any other free time. We often time enjoyed the fruits from his culinary skills at our after school sessions. I was especially fond of his pies.

His struggle was similar to training for the Olympics. Everyday mattered. You worked each day as hard as you could and then you worked some more.

His diligence and dedication transferred to others in my class and to others in the school. To those struggling, Seth became a symbol of HOPE. His progress continued on the fast-track. While he had trouble making passing grades, during his failed time in the classroom he had amassed a wealth of knowledge. When his evaluation was delivered in a different style, his true ability was exposed.

Seth went to his teachers and expressed his gratitude for their patience with him. Without the knowledge he had gathered from his time in their classrooms, his current success would not have been possible. He now had the faculty pulling for him.

By Spring Break, we could see the end. After Spring break there was just a short time until graduation week. We weren't there yet but our chances were now leaning toward success and away from failure. It was eight days before grades had to be posted when we finished. It felt great; better than either of us thought it would.

I had stood by Seth and God had guided us both. Our Mission Was Accomplished.

Being in high school for the first time, this was my first graduation. Seth was not my only student to graduate with this class and I was proud of them all, but none had touched me like he had. The counselor felt there was no accomplishment at this school to equal Seth's. Both of his parents were in the audience to cheer him on as he crossed the stage. I realized that this success navigated by God, not only was enjoyed by Seth and his family but by the whole school community.

Following the ceremony, I met most of my students' parents. I expressed to each set of parents my excitement for their student's accomplishments, and the parents all expressed their thanks for my commitment to their child.

Seth proudly introduced me to his mom and dad. He first thanked God and then introduced me as Mr. Cassady, my teacher, "My Miracle Worker."

I hope God was enjoying this as much as I was.

My thought after my first year at the high school, " I'M BACK!"

CHAPTER 26

BROKEN HEARTS

I was at the high school for six years. My program now serves several special needs students as well as providing enrichment for our honor students. It continues to provide hope for those students who are experiencing failure in the regular classroom.

I enjoyed the private, parochial setting. It was great being able to celebrate Christmas and Easter with references to the true meaning of each. It was so comforting to work in an environment where caring and praying is a part of the curriculum. The school was an educational community of faith where people actually cared about each other. I tell people that I liked my job so much that I hated to take money for it.

There was one year that was most memorable. It was a year of ups and downs. That year I called on God to intervene on numerous occasions. Personally I was a part of several life changing challenges. Our school community would also face life altering event.

That school year began a week late for me. Vicki and I were completing a two week cruise and land excursion to Alaska. We experienced the best of God's work as we enjoyed its endless, unaltered landscapes. Sprawling out before us were thousands of acres of land that had never felt the

Bridging The Gap

footsteps of man. The waters were clear and clean and provided the area with its life quenching gift. The air was pure and uncontaminated, "the breath of life." All of these elements existing in a balance, the land, the water, and the wildlife, all molded into one, by the Creator.

This was a place for you to get in touch with yourself. This was a chance to bond with each other. This was a time of appreciation of all of God's wonders. It was a time of reflection. It was a time that could last forever, but not this time.

We returned home on the Friday before Labor Day weekend. In our pile of mail collected over our two week absence, was a letter from the Northeast Oklahoma Tribal Health System marked IMORTANT. The impact of that label alone made me anxious. As I ripped the letter from the envelope; I had that feeling in the pit of my stomach that this was bad news.

A quick scan of the letter revealed an urgent request for me to return to the clinic as soon as possible. A recent EKG taken the day before we left on the cruise indicated an irregularity in my heart. Another section reported that according to the EKG, I had recently experienced a heart attack. This matter needed immediate attention to prevent further heart damage.

That was indeed unwelcomed news. Even worse was the fact that the letter was dated the day we left on our cruise vacation two weeks ago. The first opportunity I had to call, because of the Labor Day holiday, was on Tuesday. They were having a diabetic clinic all day, but I was assured a phone call by the end of the day. At 5:00 p.m. I had still not received a call.

Starting at 8:00 the next morning I continued calling. When I didn't hear from the clinic by lunch break, I took the afternoon off and drove to the clinic. I knew if I sit around their long enough, someone would eventually take care of me.

As luck would have it my doctor was not there, but I did get to visit with one of the other doctors. He said that this letter reported a very serious situation that called for a stress test and other heart related labs. These tests would have to be performed at my local hospital. The staff at the clinic made the necessary calls and I had an appointment but not until the following Monday. That was almost a month from the time the letter was sent.

The next five days were very unsettled. I knew several people who had scheduled stress tests and ended up lying in a hospital with their chest cracked open recovering from open heart surgery. That's something I feared

Once again I went one–on–one with God about this very serious situation. From our discussion I came away feeling like the survivor I was for the last forty years. I was confident that I could make the adjustments necessary to live.

As the time for the testing drew near, I actually thought about what might happen if God called me home. That would signal an end to my mission.

Mission Accomplished!

Having examined all possible outcomes, I entered the testing room on that Monday morning with a high degree of confidence. I must honestly say I was scared, but most of that was just fear of the unknown.

Two hours later the testing was complete. They told me the results would be sent to the clinic and I should make an appointment to discuss them with my primary health care provider. I knew that meant I might have to wait as long as a month to find out about them. I asked the tech in charge if I should make an appointment with a cardiologist. He told me I had nothing to worry about. If they had found anything I would have been immediately admitted to the hospital. That was the news I wanted to here. As I left the hospital with my wife, I thanked God for being beside me and bringing me through another crisis. Again I looked to the future for additional challenges.

It was two weeks before I received the results. All of the test results were good and the EKG at the hospital was clean. The personnel at the clinic admitted that it was probably just a faulty EKG. One of my students, his father was a surgeon, told me that his dad said a very high percentage of EKG's report a false positive.

The semester was not what you would imagine as it began with a trip of a lifetime cruise to Alaska. While that was great, it failed to register as the most important development of the year. Too much had happened since the beginning of the year. My scare with heart disease knocked the travel extravaganza out of the water. Then there was the recurring problem with my sight and the possible loss of vision. In the age we live in those health issues could be fixed as most things can be. Then there was the knee replacement that was scheduled for early December. That was another thing that could be fixed.

Pretty tough days, but the most important development of the first semester was the loss of Sandy, my friend and colleague. Her diagnosis with liver cancer and her immediate resignation not only changed my life, but it changed the lives of many, many young people and it cannot be fixed. Liver cancer is one of the medical mysteries that still carry a terminal diagnosis.

I first met Sandy when I was a new faculty member. After a bit of a bumpy start she became my mentor and my protector, not a bad thing to have when you're the new kid on the block. As she said, "we're a team." That November she was diagnosed with terminal liver cancer. Her final journey was short.

She was like a mother figure to me. She was just starting to open up and share. We had talked about life and death previous to her diagnosis and I had shared my experience with her. I knew that our time together was going to be much too short.

I looked at her frail figure, wasting away more and more each day. It was horrible for her, but not as horrible as her diagnosis. The assault on her liver was draining every ounce of energy she could muster.

It was a Wednesday. She had only found out about her terminal condition two days previous. She spent the entire day in her room. She wore her long wool winter coat all day long. Her skin was chalky and pale. She never left her office chair. She never left the room. She had lost 100 pounds in the last year. She sat confused and didn't know what she wanted. The diagnosis was too new. It was so final. What choice did she have?

At the end of the day she struggled to walk to the door. She carried with her a solitary box containing her personal possessions. One of those artifacts was her stapler. . . . Go Figure. As she shuffled out of her room towards the elevator she assured me that I needn't worry for her as she was going fast. She wasn't going to suffer. With those words, her frail body disappeared behind the closing elevator doors and she was gone. That's the way it was. Not Pretty. Not Happy. Just the way it was.

She was very emphatic about how she wished to be treated. She wanted no one to know, wanted no special treatment or pity. Even when I mentioned that God made us caring creatures and put us on earth to care for other people, she held to her position of just fading away.

While some thought her attitude reflected a position of giving up, I felt she was just using the time to pack up and prepare and while they have much to look forward to, the sorrow they feel is in leaving loved ones early; loved ones who are clinging to fragments of a life fully lived, hopeful for just one more memory.

One evening soon after her announcement in regard to her diagnosis I had an encounter with a bob cat. On a visit to our local nature center the cat ran in front of my car and vanished into the nearby woods. A bobcat sighting is rare for our area. In my Native American teaching the totem of the bobcat embodies the spirit of life, that same spirit we were losing through Sandy. Her spirit was being released back to the creator who will reveal her future.

My knee surgery came and went. The procedure was successful and I was soon on my feet. My first concern after I recovered from the initial trauma of the surgery was Sandy's condition. She had surgery to reduce her suffering and was in the ICU unit at the same hospital where I had been recovering. I felt she was holding on in ICU weighing the imperfections that tie her to this sinful world against a peaceful guarantee of eternity. Knowing Sandy she was probably arguing with St. Peter about her placement in line, insisting that there are many if not all who should claim their place in heaven ahead of her.

Christmas was fast approaching and December 23, Vicki and I celebrated our wedding anniversary. Early in the evening I heard the phone ring, and I knew before answering that my teaching friend and colleague had passed. The news was shocking at first, but not surprising. It was expected and it was something that I had been anticipating. Tears stained my face; I realized her journey was over.

Sleep did not come easy that night. After tossing and turning, I finally got out of bed and went to our living room. During the nights before Christmas we kept the light on the tree lit all the time. It was a beautiful and peaceful place to pray and in the early hours of Christmas Eve, I said my final farewell.

Bridging The Gap

What's missing? Way more than you would expect. Sandy represented the past, a generation of caring, thinking and dreaming. She was from a time when man did as much as possible to control his identity. She was a champion of the underdog. Missing is that person who would stay after school and visit about what was troubling you. She was an ear to listen, and a shoulder to lean on. She was a perfectionist and everything had to be done just right. That was just part of her character. Her full productive life ended with an exclamation point, and then all was gone, and life goes on.

I returned to school after Christmas Break. My recovery was not complete but I could drive, and get around well enough to complete my classroom duties. I worked with several students who needed special attention. The care and appreciation shown by the students in regard to my return helped greatly in my recovery and we all helped each other accept the sadness and sorrow we were all suffering in the wake of Sandy's passing.

At the Easter's Day service, God hinted at a new project he was calling me to undertake. At the church service, our priest spoke again about recognizing our God given talents. He spoke of special moments we experience with God in our lives. God may have provided a special experience for me but it was my duty to share it with others. Up to that point, I had shared my special times only with small groups and individuals. The sermon again left me trying to decipher God's message.

The next week, the Catholic Bishop spoke at a celebration at the school and shared the same message. I was beginning to get it. I needed to share my experiences with large groups of people. That next week I authored an internet blog, www.myawakeningmoments@blogspot.com. My first post was a summary of my heavenly experience. I followed it up with spiritual experiences that were happening all around me in daily life. I also volunteered to be a speaker at the spring Senior Retreat. At that event, following my testimony, I announced my interest in publishing this book.

That special year finally came to an end. It was one that I started out enjoying God's Glory. The remainder of the year was spent managing one difficult challenge after another. It was God's intervention that helped me through each potentially damaging crisis. In the end, God challenged me to share my experiences with the world.

I Accepted His Challenge.

CHAPTER 27

"MY JESUS OF MERCY, I TRUST IN YOU"

"My Jesus of Mercy, I Trust in You," words from The Divine Mercy Chaplet. As a student body we recited this daily. As an individual, these words give me confidence in all situations. When I hear an emergency vehicle or pass an accident scene, I recite those words.

Jesus promises, "The souls that say the chaplet will be embraced by My mercy during their life time and especially at the hour of their death. When the chaplet is said in the presence of the dying, I will stand between My Father and the dying person, not as the judge, but as the Merciful Savior."

Those words represent the contents of this book. I didn't learn the words of the Devine Mercy Chaplet until I began my tenure at the church school. I found that trust forty years ago when God showed me his plan, when he revealed eternity. Since that time I try to live that life of trust. When you live in a world where sin surrounds you it is natural to drift off the spiritual path but just ask and God, as your guide, will give direction to your journey.

When you stray far, or get lost along the way, Christ will restore you with hope and confidence and strengthen your Faith.

I taught at the parochial high school for six years. There are many times that I am thankful for that work. It provided an additional income to help support my pitiful money management problem. More importantly it reminded me each day of why we as humans exist on this imperfect planet. It gave me a chance to affect the future.

When people walked through the halls of that school they recognized right away that they were in a different place. I was proud that school was different. I felt that there was no better tribute to Sandy than to continue the school's tradition; continuing to be the highly regarded parochial school for which it was founded.

Outside of school, family remains a priority. Vicki and I attend church and we enjoy seeing our daughters work in the church. We enjoy watching Cal and Wil grow up in the church. We especially enjoy their helpful, caring attitude in regard to family and for those in need. Our daughters continue their careers in education.

When we gather for family events, education always has its place at the family table. Our discussions are not so much about the success and failures of particular students but more so about what represents success and failure. How do you ensure success and wipe out failure? We also like to vacation as a family and truly have fun just being together.

The Joplin tornado brought us closer as a family. While we were not directly affected we are able to reflect on our personal past tornado experiences. Our area grew as a community, and our churches grew as a community of faith. The catastrophic event gave us all a chance to reach out to those in need. I truly believe that through the tornado and the recovery efforts God touched the lives of more of the people that I know than any other single event in my lifetime.

I continue to pray for those who suffered the loss of family members and loved ones. I continue to pray for those who lost their home and personal belongings. It has been a true story of "resurrection" to watch the devastated areas come back to life.

I continue to attend the Episcopal Church where I have been a parishioner for more than forty years. I continue to receive comfort from the liturgy and guidance and spiritual strength from the sermons. I serve as an usher welcoming the old and encouraging the new who venture through the doors of our church. I always enjoy a friendly comment of appreciation for my former service to the church.

I look forward to a time when I can share "my experience" to a large "community of faith" with confidence.

My father remains a mystery. While we live only fifteen miles apart, I may go for months without seeing him. We talk on the phone occasionally but it has been years since he has visited with me and my family in our home. Recently we have participated in scaled back family functions at his house.

I feel that the loss of my mother was too much for him. I feel that he still wrestles with guilt issues. He can't let go. It seems that he is using my brother and me as a shield between my mother and him.

He lives with a wonderful women Sue, and she cares a great deal for him. They take care of each other. They keep each other from being lonely, otherwise I would worry. I pray daily that he can find PEACE.

I continue my interest in American Indian issues. Being born one-fourth Native American I have recently become more interested in the activities of my tribe. There was a time in my life when I wrestled with the native beliefs compared to Christian beliefs.

It was another one of those spiritual battles of the heart and mind. Through prayer I was guided to an understanding that we as Christians should look for the similarities of spiritual beliefs opposed to the differences. This should apply not only to tribal beliefs but should extend to all cultures and religious denominations.

I can't complete this project without acknowledging my thoughtful, devoted wife Vicki. She has been the perfect counterpart for me as I traveled along my spiritual path. We laugh together and we cry together. We share pride for accomplishments and we share sorrow in times of failure and tragedy. She is a tremendously caring person who divides her time among her numerous passions. I owe my successes to her patience and support.

As for the future, I hope to write an additional volume that will introduce you to more of the specific challenges God placed along my spiritual path. It will be a collection of short character sketches of those who contributed to my spiritual journey.

In conclusion I offer three words: Faith, Hope, and Love. As you continue on your own spiritual journey, remember, Faith, Hope and Love Conquers All.

May your journey be fruitful and may the Peace of the Lord be with you.

AFTERWARDS

Ten years have passed since I finished the last pages of the first edition of Bridging the Gap, A Spiritual Journey to Heaven and Back. Each year, life becomes more challenging. As always God is with me to provide guidance and support to help me navigate the day by days.

My first stop on my continued journey was at the local university. I was called to teach two classes in the International Student's Department, collaborating with young men and women from the middle east and from China. It was a wake-up call for me to realize the differences in lifestyles in diverse cultures. Spiritual customs and beliefs were especially interesting to me. My job was to help these young first-year students adjust to the region as they become acclimated to college life in America, especially Southwest Missouri. Since our time together was the fall semester, they were able to experience Thanksgiving and Christmas holidays and they were all eager to participate. Our time together was a learning experience. I tried my best to present our culture and lifestyles simply as tools to help them maneuver the American system of higher education. In the brief time I was together with these young adults our culture sharing event broadened my view of world politics and influenced my empathy for international events that would follow.

One of the most notable events during his time was the loss of my father. He was a healthy, fit man until he wasn't. Suddenly life stopped working for him. As he aged his heart became weak as did his kidneys.

When we finally got him to a doctor, tests revealed that he had experienced a series of small heart attacks which caused permanent damage. As is often the case with congestive heart failure, the kidneys also suffer. It happened so quickly. He became confused and depressed.

He had lived a healthy life. What went wrong?

The doctor told us that if he had set on his couch two more days he would have died. Because his family stood with him and because his medical team was quick to diagnose and quick to act, Dad borrowed more days. When he left his house that afternoon in December, I knew he would not return. As his medical condition began to improve, he was assigned to a nursing home.

My dad was very independent and became cynical in his old age. My concern was he would refuse treatment and just die. He rallied and for his last 80 days; he was a new man. My one wish for my gravely ill father was that he would live long enough to understand the goodness of humanity. That miracle was achieved; my father was greenlighted to begin his new life with his Heavenly Father. My dad fought hard but as his days ended, I knew he was a fighter, but he just got a better offer. Losing a loved one is always sad, but how can you expect a loved one to turn down the offer of eternity?

The next year, to the date I lost my father-in-law. My faith was again challenged but as with my father, he was ready for a new adventure.

As it is with God, as one travels through time of darkness, we are always moving toward the light. In the early summer, my youngest daughter, Sarah was married to Jason Brunner and with the marriage we became instant grandparents to two additional grandboys, Jackson and Jordon. A year later I hosted a family cruise to Alaska. This activity allowed new family members to bond and opened the door to a bright future.

My introduction to mass shootings occurred while on a trip to Las Vegas on tribal business. Immediately after we landed and began our cab ride to the hotel. A shooter at a nearby hotel opened fire on a large group attending a concert. As our driver approached the area of the active shooter, thousands of concert goers flooded into the street running for their lives. Shots flew overhead, penetrating giant jet fuel tanks, some ricocheting off the steel containers. When we reached the hotel, it was locked down behind us.

I entered the dark hotel room; the bright lights from the Las Vegas strip filtered through the uncovered windows. That light lured me to the glass. I pulled up a chair and a set quietly staring up and down Las Vegas Blvd. There were no people, no cars, no limos, no buses, just empty sidewalks. The only traffic was emergency vehicles blazing trails of red and blue throughout the early morning darkness. The streets were vacant, all of Vegas was locked down. I realized I was alone and unsure of what had happened. I turned on the TV. By now it was almost 2:00 in the morning and all the local news outlets were fully engaged in this story of the tragedy.

Darkness settled over the concert venue. Hidden beneath the darkness of that early morning was the remains of sixty innocent concert attendees. More than four hundred were treated at local hospitals.

I was sick to my stomach. I felt sadness, sympathy, and anger all at once. I rushed to the opened curtains and closed them tight. I closed the blackout curtains. I wanted it all blacked out.

As I lay in bed that early morning staring at the red light on the smoke alarm I continued to try and process what had happened. Even though I was encased in my room, all outside blocked out I could not forget. In that early morning I stressed about what to do. It was in those moments that I released my soul, my spirit to carry a message of Love to all concerned. Love is the beginning of all healing. The sound of emergency vehicles continued up and down Las Vegas Blvd, sirens wailing against the quiet of early morning and leaving the unknown on your mind while sleep happened.

Since being a part of the mass shooting in Vegas, the world is still a dangerous place. Since that event, many other mass shootings have occurred. Not much has happened to make one feel more secure or safer, we just have bigger hearts and an abundance of faith.

Immediately after returning from Vegas, I was diagnosed with prostate cancer.

Cancer is an unabridged subject. The very reference to the word is debilitating to the mind as well as the body. The thought of cancer cells growing inside of me numbed my brain and hampered my thoughts for the future. I have never felt so helpless, yet so angry and so hostile, all at one time.

It fills every moment of consciousness, a full-time battle. I was consumed by an unknown enemy that held my very existence in its sweaty palms. Is this representation a bit too dramatic?

Not at all!!

The first time the word was used in my diagnosis I gasped for breath and had to fight back throwing up. A comforting wife's caring pat on my back calmed me and interrupted the harsh spiral that saw a world with less of me, less of my wife, my children, and my grandchildren. I prepared to face a great, scary unknown.

What kind of future do I have to look forward to, too?

Once again, I am a survivor. There are more days. I am alive to serve.

What do you say about Covid? For two years you awoke to another ground hog's day. No answers. No truths. No responsibility. Just more sickness, more deaths. No amount of arguing, no amount of blame, ended the sickness and death. Death and sickness touched us all.

I again, on many occasions, invoked the freeing of my spirit and my soul. That was the only prescription that brought me Peace.

Two final stories, one showing the good in the world; the other an example of how evil slips in and can cloud decision making.

First thing every day for fifteen months I would check Facebook to see if there were new posts chronicling a youngster in our community who was battling stage four cancer. It was a rare form, so unique that St. Jude's Children's Hospital could do nothing to help.

Just days after the diagnosis, the community rallied behind the cause, and within weeks there were thousands following this eleven-year-old boy with bright, inciteful eyes and a huge, welcoming smile.

It was my pleasure to be a part of the immense prayer group that measured thousands and became socially knitted into an active community of faith stretching from coast to coast.

From the beginning, the prognosis was terminal, but through prayer, thousands of comments of encouragement, the boy named Christian remained strong and in the fight until the very end.

As his dad reported, "Christian had the body of a youngster with the old soul of a mature Christian.

The body of a 14-year-old boy from Afghanistan was found dead, the apparent result of a suicide. The youngster, a part of a group of Afgan refugees resettled in a conservative southwest Missouri community. He was found hanging at the high school's baseball field.

The death of a student on school property should always have a place in the hearts and minds of fellow students. Did the students know? What did the students know? Was this a subject of discussion at local churches? How was this received by local teens? How did it fit into youth group discussions?

All is quiet. It is easier to forget something that is not real. There is no guilt in something you don't know about.

Early accounts of the incident reported that privacy for the family was the reason for lack of information.

Suicide is one of the leading causes of teen deaths in America today. It is managed with sensitivity, but communities understand their role in working with the family to help them through challenging times. This community should be no different.

Official Report. The hanging victim was found on school property early in the morning before school started. Authorities were notified. School and police suggest that no further reports were filed at the request of the family to protect privacy. Bullying was suggested as a cause for the actions of the youngster. Police and school bristled at that suggestion countering that not a single student had come forward to report bullying. Three weeks had passed.

How do you report on a case that hasn't been acknowledged?

Bullying or no bullying at school, the fact is, a Go-fund-me account set up by citizens of the community with the specific purpose of the relocation of this family.

There was one member of the administrative team that posted on his private FB page, a very guarded post about love and kindness and children.

How many did this shameful cover-up touch? These are good people, good Christians. My prayers are for all who were collateral damage in this experience and especially for those who chose that path for the celebration of the life for a human child.

Too often, doing the right thing comes with giant consequences and hurdles to overcome before you even reach the root of the problem.

I have overcome giant problems in my life.

God must be the driver of your plan, and a tight web must exist to weed out the evil. I know it surrounds me 24-7 and it is present in all possibilities, in all persons and in all places. Prayer is my weapon. I shall add warrior to my survivor label.

Keep believing, keep praying, and keep loving. Catch you later!

-Calvin

ABOUT THE AUTHOR

Calvin Cassady is a retired school teacher. His career in education spanned more than thirty-five years and included assignments in both private and public schools. While working with youngsters of all ages he took every opportunity to present himself as a Christian role model and through his education ministry many successes were realized.

He served as a church leader for more than fifteen years. During this time he was responsible for the Christian education and youth events at his local Episcopal Church. Presenting Christ through his experiences made a positive difference for many young people that his message touched.

Calvin is a Native American and an active member of the Seneca-Cayuga tribe of Oklahoma. He has researched his tribal heritage and enjoys his cultural diversity.

He is a strong supporter of environmental and ecological education. Sharing the wonder of all that God has created is an important part of his mission. He has served on the boards of the Wildcat Glades Conservation and Audubon Center, the Ozark Gateway Audubon Society, and the state board for Missouri Master Naturalists.

Calvin lives in a small southwest Missouri community with his wife Vicki and his five cats. He enjoys spending time with his daughters, Sarah, and Rebecca and her husband Brett. Calvin and Wilson, the grandchildren are a constant reminder of Mr. Cassady's mission and a notice that the journey goes on.

Printed in the USA
CPSIA information can be obtained
at www.ICGtesting.com
JSHW022053080823
46188JS00003B/26